Diabetes among the Pima

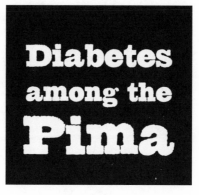

Stories of Survival

Carolyn Smith-Morris

The University of Arizona Press
Tucson

The University of Arizona Press
© 2006 The Arizona Board of Regents
All rights reserved

This book is printed on acid-free, archival-quality paper.
Manufactured in the United States of America

11 10 09 08 07 06   6 5 4 3 2 1

Library of Congress Cataloging-in-Publication Data
Smith-Morris, Carolyn, 1966–
Diabetes among the Pima : stories of survival /
Carolyn Smith-Morris.
p. cm.
Includes bibliographical references and index.
ISBN-13: 978-0-8165-2553-9 (hardcover : alk. paper)
ISBN-10: 0-8165-2553-6 (hardcover : alk. paper)
1. Diabetes—Arizona. 2. Diabetes in pregnancy—
Arizona. 3. Diabetics—Medical care—Arizona.
4. Pima Indians—Health and hygiene. 5. Pima Indians
—Diseases. I. Title.
RA645.D5 S55 2006
616.4′6200899745529—dc22
                              2006006333

Dedicated to Robert P. Smith and Cecelia T. Smith

Contents

Illustrations

Figures

Tables

Acknowledgments

I am most grateful to the women of Gila River who shared their lives and pregnancies with me. Their warm and enthusiastic welcome made this a wholly gratifying experience, and I value their friendships. I also thank the elders and leaders at Gila River, particularly the Gila River Community Council and its Health and Social Committee, for their guidance, constructive criticism, and encouragement.

The work would not have been possible without the financial support of the National Science Foundation (#9910441), the Wenner-Gren Foundation (#6502), and the Agency for Health Care Quality and Research (#R03HS10802). But I want also to acknowledge the smaller awards that supported early phases of the research: an Edward H. Spicer Scholarship for Research in the Southwest and Northern Mexico (University of Arizona) and an Arizona Archaeological and Historical Society Scholarship (Arizona State Museum).

I also remain gratefully indebted to my advisors at the University of Arizona: Ana Ortiz, Mark Nichter, Susan Philips, Jennie Joe, and Tom Weaver. And to that crucial second line of support in times of dire need: M. E. Morbeck, Steven Zegura, and Bill Longacre. There are many colleagues as well, for whose time and thoughts I am indebted, but particularly Dan Benyshek, Brooke Olson, Christopher Tillquist, Dennis Weidman, and Gretchen Lang.

Finally, thanks to my family and friends, who were simultaneously support, critics, editors, and assistants. To Lauren, who attended every interview without fail, in utero; to Cecelie, who bore the most painful of field scars, second-degree burns to her hand at an off-reservation, unshaded playground; to Kelly for heroism on all counts, but especially for fixing the swamp coolers, for fishing the live lizard out of the toilet, and for keeping a great sense of humor throughout; and to Dad, my favorite and principal editor.

Part I

1

Diabetes *Ho'ok*

Living with a Witch

The child . . . settled and grew up south of here somewhere in Papago country. From then, whenever she found that there was a baby at some place, she would go there and play very kindly with it, take the baby home, and eat it up. All the people were afraid, so they let her take their babies. (From Morning Green Chief and the Witch, the Pima creation narrative in Bahr et al. 1994:143)

In the thousand-year civilization of the Hohokam, forerunners of the Sonoran Desert people now called the Pima, people spoke of a predator who ate children. This predator was female and Hohokam by birth, so not a stranger but a neighbor to the Pimas. They called her a *ho'ok,* a witch. She would find a baby at some place, play very kindly with it, take the baby home, and "eat it up." The parents did not resist, because they were so afraid.

Generations of Pimas have faced a similar predator in the diabetes epidemic that kills them at a rate four times that of white Americans. It can quietly affect Pima babies in the womb, only later to eat them up through infections and heart and renal disease. The disease grips more than half of all Pimas by adulthood, and its prevalence is still on the rise. Here's how the people describe it (all names are pseudonyms):

Laura: Talking about it, this hurts me, you know. His body started shutting down, and he got on dialysis. And then he had an ulcer or something . . . and they found out that he was getting an infection under his foot. And he had, I don't remember what else. So they sent him to Tucson, and they amputated up to his knee. And so then he had to get a prosthesis. And, you know, he couldn't ever, he never gained the strength to get back. I think he gave up from that point. He gave up.

Caroline: My best friend's grandmother, I was real close to her, she died because of her diabetes. She had to take insulin shots. She took them every day, and she got one blister on her foot, and they amputated and amputated until the whole leg was gone. Then they were going to amputate the next one, and that's when she gave up and just died.

Maureen: I have been diabetic for quite some time. . . . I know infection has a lot to do with your blood sugar and other things. And my amputation came because, that other complex I lived in, the neighbor didn't want to . . . get involved. And my mother didn't live too near at the time, and she was on vacation. And I had to wait until she came. . . . And so by the time I got to the doctor, you know, I didn't have a choice.

Like the Hohokam predator, diabetes comes by stealth. This is particularly so for women, who are vulnerable to the most insidious form of the disease—diabetes during pregnancy. Gestational diabetes is most often symptomless, disappears after childbirth, yet leaves both the mother and infant at greater risk for outright diabetes later on. The characteristic and understandable response to testing of the Pima woman, candidate for diagnosis because she is Pima, is quietude. Whether by ignorance or denial, she may feel undamaged and intact. Meanwhile, diabetes lurks inside, imprinting itself on both her and her fetus.

It is not surprising, then, that the etiology of diabetes, increasingly clear to scientists, is still murky to many pregnant women. Angela's words illustrate:

Angela: I don't know, but they tell me and they tell us in the, over there, the hospital—they tell us how you get it. I mean, how it works. And I don't remember how you get it. I mean, maybe, probably—I don't know. I don't know how it works.

Diabetes has been explained to Angela more than once, but it's still obscure to her and not something she often talks about. Indeed, despite such a long history in the community, few people talk about it. The public dialogue about diabetes is largely about its obscurity, which is both natural and socially imposed.

Laura: They just give up, but a lot of people, that's why we don't talk about diabetes. It wasn't talked about much when I was growing up. It was, like, taboo. It's the disease that had a really bad stigmatism [*sic*] to its name.

As if talk of it would conjure it into existence, diabetes is taboo. Decades of effort to curb the epidemic have failed, giving Pimas the impression that it is impenetrable and immovable.

> **Sara:** I read it that Pimas have, you know, have a real high risk . . . more than anybody else. You know . . . so that's what I think . . . it's just how Pimas are.

It's just how Pimas are.

Diabetes' lack of symptoms explains much of the fear and inaction that is plain in the behavior of Pimas. This is true for many people with diabetes, not just Pimas. When I asked the Pimas who wouldn't go to the doctor, several women gave the same types of response: they're afraid of the diagnosis.

> **Fay:** I guess they're afraid of what's gonna happen or what they're gonna say or are they gonna get sick more. . . . They think, you know, like I remember my mom: before she died she never went to the hospital, she wasn't gonna go. . . . To her it was like if you go to the doctor, you know, you get sick more.

> **Alma:** Scared of what they're gonna find out, or some probably just don't want to. Like a couple people I know they just never went [to the doctor] cause they're like, they don't want to know or whatever.

> **Dorothy:** I don't know. What I see is that they know that they're gonna be diabetic.

Fay, Alma, and Dorothy bespeak a Pima fear that medical attention will confirm—if it does not actually give you—diabetes. Given that fear, their reticence is not surprising. But from the perspective of the biomedical clinician, Fay, Alma, and Dorothy address the apathy, futility, and denial that are all too characteristic of the Pima population. In biomedical canon, patients have an obligation to avoid disease, to do what they can to get better, and to resist death to the very end. They are to perform their sick role (Parsons 1971), in which apathy and denial have no place.

This difference in perspective is not simply about the avoidability of diabetes; it is a conflict in worldview. For clinicians, the prevention, diagnosis, and treatment of a disease are paramount. For Pimas, health is more a function of living well than of bodily vigilance. Pimas believe in good health, but many are convinced that the way to achieve it is by avoiding an obsession with its fine details. The logistic barriers alone are enough to deter many from treatment. But if diabetes has no symptoms that one can recognize as pathological, then the inquiry itself is the principal—if not the only—pathology. To submit is to become a hypochondriac.

For those who study this epidemic, diabetes in the Pima people is a convergence of genetic, historical, cultural, and environmental influences. Nearly 40 years of intensive clinical research at Gila River by the National Institutes of Health has produced sophisticated diagnostic measures, life-extending medications, and much of the world's knowledge about diabetes and its impact on the body. Several NIH researchers have been working in and near Gila River for longer than some of my informants have been alive. Yet a long history of rational, empirical methods has made the investigation itself part of the Pima pathology. The failure of biomedicine and science to develop a cure for diabetes has left many Pimas skeptical and even suspicious about the worth of further inquisition into their lives and bodies.

This skepticism was brought home to me during a tribal council meeting on health issues—the first Health and Social Committee meeting that I had attended.[1] There to propose his new clinical study on a diabetes-related problem, a research physician spoke first. His project required the taking of tissue samples from a number of Pima volunteers. He delivered a professionally prepared booklet to each councilman and addressed them with projected slides and a clear and convincing explanation of the project and its clinical importance. The doctor then waited for questions and what he (and I) clearly expected to be a vote for approval.

There was a long pause. The councilmen stared down at their pages. Then a single question: "Will it hurt when you take this sample?" "Only a little," the doctor replied casually. Next, the chair called for the vote, and the committee voted summarily to reject the project. One councilman went further, scolding the bewildered physician for his colleagues' failure to report their findings from another, previous study. "Why hasn't Dr. X (the head of the research group) come in person?" It was a long, uncomfortable moment for the physician. The audience of 20 people sat aghast, none more so than I, who was next on the agenda for a proposal of my own research.

I had spent almost three years in preparation for that day. I volunteered at the Diabetes Education Center (DEC) in the tribal hospital.[2] I began to make friends and contacts, talking with employees about diabetes and doing research in the community. Few Pimas had heard of my kind of "talking" research (i.e., ethnography). Most found it puzzling, and certainly of little threat, and they sensed it would allow Pimas to tell the story their own way. These new friends led me to community leaders and elders, to the district meetings around the reservation, to the hospital board of directors, and to the tribal health advisory board. In this seemingly endless series of meetings, each person or group suggested one or two others who'd want to "have a look at it." Was I being given the runaround? A number of other researchers and clinicians had told me how Pimas would send you someplace else rather than deliver a direct and provocative refusal. Perhaps, as I thought many times over these three years, all my networking would lead nowhere, and I'd be refused permission to stay.

I would eventually come to a different opinion about this piling on of additional reviews. It dawned on me that this might be a cultural remnant from precolonial times, a process of consensus decision making. Had any significant problem or popular criticism appeared during my two and a half years of volunteer work at the hospital and almost six months of formal permission seeking, the project would have been rejected. The Pimas thus achieved a traditionally sound decision by broad review and consensual approval.

I did receive endorsement by the Health and Social Committee that day, and later by the full tribal council. One thing cemented my good standing before these bodies. I had been seen by the leaders in social settings on the reservation—a family memorial, a crystal party (like an Avon or Tupperware party), a parade, errands to the grocery store and Texaco, babysitting, doing laundry, and so on. In such contexts, I could hear Pimas talk:

> **Mary:** I think its just kind of a personal thing. . . . I don't talk to my grandmother about it (laughs).
> **CS-M:** Have you talked to anybody about the tests you're doing?
> **Mary:** Yes, the doctors . . .
> **CS-M:** But, anyone in your family?
> **Mary:** Oh no! . . .

New friends and their families received me warmly, as if my presence, even at intimate family affairs like the one-year memorial of a man I'd never met, was not only acceptable but somehow a pleasant surprise to them. Children escorted me to the food tables, pointing out the better fry bread, insisting I load up my plate as they had done, steering me past the salad and toward the desserts. Out of respect for their welcome, I stifled my ethnographic noisiness and let my sponsors suggest the activity, pace, and topic.

At this slower pace—Indian time—I ingratiated myself. My network spoke volumes about my intentions. The exasperation of the councilmen with the physician researcher before me—their suspicion, their unwillingness to invest the slightest pain in mere analysis—all of this confirmed my impression that the ethnographic route into Pima diabetes would reveal something different and important.

The story of diabetes at Gila River might begin from any one of three time periods: prehistoric, historic, or contemporary. But because the influences on Pima diabetes span millennia, a meaningful snapshot of Pimas' experience today must also be a narrative reflecting all three periods. This ethnography is such a snapshot. The first of the three time periods is a prehistoric frame, during which important distinguishing features of the Pima genetic code were forming. The Pimas have lived in Southern Arizona for at least 500 years, and they consider themselves descendants of the ancient Hohokam who occupied southern and central Arizona for about 1,100 years, between AD 400 and AD 1500 (Bahti and Bahti 1997; Fagan 1995). Relevant are archaeological data, the banks of evidence on North American peopling routes, ecology, adaptation, and diversity in the smallest molecules. What of those early travelers, their lives, how they negotiated life amidst predators? It was with these visions in mind that I first approached the contemporary Pima Indians, in whose veins surge the same genetic data informing the treatises of Szathmary and Wendorf. Could Pima narratives bring the cold, hard, Beringean genetic code to life?

Second is the historic period, speaking to the political and economic factors behind modern rates of diabetes, including colonization of this area and the culture change experienced by Native Americans. In the middle and late 1800s, the Pima were trusted scouts and providers of grain for the U.S. Army (e.g., Ortiz 1973). By the late nineteenth century, however, almost all of the Pima farms were dry. This loss of water and land, the Pima's development of dependency on the federal government for food, and the eventual resurgence of Pima autonomy and self-sufficiency have mirrored the experience of many

Native American groups. Indeed, diseases of development, incomplete development, and marginalization of the poor are also paradigms amply illustrated at Gila River.

The third period is the contemporary one, within which Pimas lived their lives and spoke to me about them. I accessed this period primarily through women's narratives, and it receives the largest share of attention in this volume. Talk about illness—termed *illness narratives*—has always been a part of medical anthropology. Illness narratives are situated, limited, and socially strategic accounts. We consider illness narratives more than a simple story: they are a way for speakers to manage new information or experiences, to prepare accounts that are appropriate for a specific audience or context, and, some argue, to impact what is going on in an illness experience (e.g., Farmer 1994; Garro 1994; Good and Del Vecchio Good 1994; Kleinman 1985; Lang 1989).

Through conversations with a variety of women for hours at a time, "local" interpretations of diabetes and prenatal care, though not homogeneous, became apparent. The interview questions unified the general direction of women's stories but were not specific or limiting enough to preclude great variability. In a similar vein, interviewing pregnant women up to three and four times during their pregnancy permitted different experiences and different interpretations to surface. Criticisms and negativity were more likely to be expressed later in our relationships than within the first hour or two. And, as with the telling and retelling of any story, these women "brought to life" a version of themselves and others that would help them know how to act in the future (Capps and Ochs 1995:175).

This approach to interview data addresses "what the 'ways of speaking' . . . can reveal about the representation of cultural knowledge" (Hill 1989:66). Considerations of language and illness typically focus on lexical categories of disease and, in the more Marxist considerations, the historical and ideological factors producing those categories. Thus, two temporal frames (contemporary and historic) are blended in women's language. The third, prehistoric frame might be said to impact Pimas more covertly, continuously, at a cellular level. As this introduction already implies, my chosen route into Pima diabetes was through the narratives of Pima mothers. These women face the predator. They are not fooled by its trickery, and many recognize its obscured form in their own wombs.

It is my goal to fairly represent women's strategies for facing diabetes, and to address their place in the struggle against rising prevalence rates. I give special attention to the discursive tools and dialectic structures that guide the practice of healing. Pima women's accounts reveal how specific terms—for example, "risk" and "borderline diabetes"—and several aspects of interaction—that is, the physician's gaze and style of interaction—have a profound impact on their understanding of disease, and on their willingness and ability to access care.

The exploitation of women as the carriers of diabetes has yet to reach its pinnacle. The future promises to be increasingly medicalized and surveilled for the pregnant women of Gila River, for reasons I hope are apparent in this book. If my discussion evaluates a process of health care surveillance not yet complete, what then are the implications for action? Can policy change be productive now, informing a more community-based and proactive approach before the brunt of diabetes prevention descends on pregnant women? Or is greater responsibility for the escalating epidemic inevitable for already stigma- and blame-avoidant women? By making an argument about the symbolic potential of current prevention approaches, I am speaking beyond the events and relationships that exist now at Gila River. That is, I do not place blame for hegemonic events on the hunched shoulders of providers and patients at Gila River. To be sure, there is blame in this book—residents blaming clinicians and researchers, and vice versa, for this problem. But there is far more creativity and proactivity at Gila River, and in spite of my representational omissions, this point should be clear.

The people of Gila River—both the residents and the predominantly non-Indian professionals that call this place their occupational home—are neither shy about nor unfamiliar with the need for drastic change. Change in the diabetes rates is necessary, agreed to by all. But the onus and site for that change are the points of contention. Ideally, there will be enough collectivity and insurgency to withstand the momentum of this growing epidemic.

Today's diabetes scourge at Gila River is the culmination of generations lived in the Sonoran Desert. It is coded into the cell and habituated into life. As a disease passed down, diabetes not only reflects the relationship between the generations but characterizes it. Women are inevitably linchpins in this process for their role in reproduction. So gestational diabetes is not just about the one woman, but about her mother and grandmother, her daughter and granddaughter. In the end of the story I quoted at the front of this chapter, it took all the people's effort to kill that predator. The people came together, using the guidance and strong medicine that Siuupu (a god) had to offer, and burned that witch in a cave. People coming together will likewise promise an end to the diabetes epidemic.

2

Getting Started

The upper Sonoran Desert near Phoenix swelters for seven months out of the year, with summer temperatures regularly at 115°F. The annual rainfall of eight to sixteen inches arrives mostly in the torrential monsoons around August. Yet this starkly inhospitable place teams with over 2,000 species of plants. Survivors like these have developed desensitized and armored bodies. The trees here are cactus, sprouting spines rather than leaves, to minimize surface exposure. Burrowing and nocturnal creatures abound, while grazers languish. The cicada is a desert insect known for its loud, buzzing call that seems to emanate from all around, camouflaging the exact whereabouts of its producer. Cicadas are particularly well adapted to the desert heat: they germinate underground, waiting up to 17 years for ideal conditions before they hatch. They fly only when desert temperatures get hot, and so exploit parts of the day shunned by their predators.

Humans likewise have made adaptations to the rigors of desert life in which the steering wheel is untouchable and the seatbelt buckle can produce a first-degree burn. Through their swamp coolers, humans have devised a cheap and effective way of adding cooling water vapor to the hot, dry atmosphere. The swamp cooler's fan blows the hot, dry desert air over wet pads and into the house, reducing the indoor temperature by up to 25°F. During the interminable August heat, sojourners without a swamp cooler can resort to frequent cold showers, a personal version of that cooling mechanism to which I resorted at the beginning of my fieldwork.

"It's getting hot to walk, yeah it's getting hot to walk," said one Pima woman in her forties. She meant that it was too hot to walk to her doctor's appointment. However, in the hottest months, when a

25° reduction still leaves the house in the nineties, even indoor activities like cooking must be adjusted:

> **Maureen:** Yeah, in school we had the basic food groups. I remember that. And there's times when I forget. . . . [I've been] getting away from those habits being here in town. There's a lot of fast food—easy, you know. I don't want to cook. It's hot.

During these hottest months, however, the human response more closely matches that of the cicada, avoiding the hostile environment rather than trying to change it. Staying put is the most important defense against the heat, so few people are moving around outside; they stay home. Home for many young, pregnant women is their parents' household. With or without their mates, young mothers often remain with parents for financial and child-care support. Housing is scarce here, so multiple generations crowd into a single home without complaint. The tribe builds housing[1] for members on a first-come-first-served basis, and the waiting list for these homes is long. One Pima mother moved her family to a rented apartment near my house while their new one was being built. She had waited several years for construction to begin, and two more years passed before the house was finished.

Though tales of desert heat may fit better in the writings of Barbara Kingsolver and Willa Cather, they are relevant to Pima women in pregnancy. Pima women approach diabetes with a different mindset—even a different body-set—for the heat, how to pass time, and comforts like food and space. Theirs is more than summertime discomfort during pregnancy. The mind-set that Kozak calls surrender and the body-set that Bourdieu calls habitus are both at work. Pima women incorporate into their pregnancies a generations-long attitude of tolerance, resilience, and bodily desensitization—the necessary armor for life in the desert.

A Pima's body-mind armor deflects a variety of bodily symptoms —thirst, swelling, fatigue. Normal reactions to the dry Sonoran heat, these are also common symptoms of diabetes—excessive thirst (and frequent urination), swelling in the extremities, and fatigue. In a conversation about her diet, a young pregnant woman named Catherine talked about her constant thirst. She said she got thirsty more often because of the heat. She also had a ferocious sweet tooth and ate candy and drank nondiet sodas whenever she could get them. She talked at length about how pregnancy worsened her sweet tooth, referring to "cravings" that, because they were produced by the baby growing inside her, she felt justified in satiating. So while she increased her consumption of liquids as instructed by her doctor, she was drinking Coke and Dr Pepper, not water. Thus, what might have been increasing thirst from diabetes, Catherine ascribed to the rising summer heat. Diabetes arrives by stealth.

Second only to the heat for its influence on daily life at Gila River is unemployment. Unemployment on many Indian reservations is high. In the 2000 census, when 3.7 percent of the U.S. labor force was unemployed, 11 percent of the Pima labor force was unemployed. Hidden behind this already striking difference is further information about how many people are actually seeking work: 64 percent of the U.S. population was in the labor force (that is, either employed or looking for work). Among Pima Indians, it was only 46 percent.

Combining the number of Pimas who were unemployed with those not looking for work yields almost 60 percent of the population without their own income (U.S. Census Bureau 2000).[2] In the dominant U.S. culture, we might generalize about workers' access to jobs: if there are no jobs in one's own town, the job seeker commutes or moves to wherever the jobs are. Employment tends to take priority over proximity to birthplace and extended family. But for the Pima, whose town is her reservation where there are relatively few jobs, moving one's home is culturally problematic if not practically impossible. Even commuting presumes car ownership. Family ties are strong, and the sense of place and home prohibits the mobility more common in the dominant culture.

Unemployment, like the heat (and like diabetes), is something that seems to belong to the reservation, "something that's with us." Only 5 percent of pregnant women I spoke to had jobs, and only a few more were actively seeking work. These figures support the census statistics. Pregnant women rely on kin networks (e.g., the income of a spouse or other family member) or various forms of government assistance for survival. Meredith's priorities are much like those of every other woman I spoke with: caring for children, filling time during the day when children are at school, and managing the heat:

CS-M: How do you spend most of the day?
Meredith: How do I spend it? First thing in the morning send my kids off to school. Spend about like a whole hour to myself, until

everybody wakes up. When they all wake up then they eat. We [Meredith and her children] eat before everybody does, so we'll, then we'll kick back, watch movies, do whatever. Bum around the rest of the day.

CS-M: Yeah, until the kids get home?

Meredith: M-hm. And what do we do? Start yelling around at the kids, and send them out, "go play outside." [We] have to get them out of our way in order for us to do what we got to do.

CS-M: And dinnertime's about what time?

Meredith: Between 5 and 6. We start doing what we gotta do, cook, feed the kids, feed everybody, and then the rest of the time we kick back, watch some more TV again, or somebody comes around. Most of the time somebody will come and visit.

CS-M: Do you go out visiting much?

Meredith: No. They come over here. Too hot for a pregnant lady.

Spending time with other family members in the house is a prominent feature of each day. It is into this landscape of (in)activity that the exhortations of medical professionals fall: "increase your exercise," "eat more vegetables and fruits," and "monitor your blood several times a day." How might women accommodate these priorities in light of the heat, their typically low or limited income, and the unemployment rates on the reservation? One way, Meredith's way, is through the comforts of time with family and the solace of food. Even when the heat wanes, and with it the reclusiveness it fosters, social activities continue to define daily life. Food holds the central place in many of these gatherings.

To heat and unemployment, then, is added a third focal point: food. Getting healthy foods on the reservation is also a challenge. Sacaton boasts a general store that stocks groceries, a few school supplies, and some hardware (nails, lightbulbs, but no replacement pads for evaporative coolers). Its kitchen serves breakfast and lunch. The gas stations in Casa Blanca and Gila Crossing offer smaller food marts. In these stores, the prices are high and the variety of fresh fruits and vegetables limited. In Appendix A, I provide a small basket comparison of Sacaton market prices with a supermarket in nearby Coolidge, itself a small-economy farming town. Some prices were higher in Coolidge than on the reservation (e.g., white bread), but, as expected, most prices were higher in Sacaton. In the winter of 1999, oats in the Sacaton market cost 13 percent more than in Coolidge;

peanut butter, 9 percent more; ground beef, 10 percent more; and cucumbers, 82 percent more. Browsers rarely visit the produce section of the Sacaton market, although lines of people await burgers and breakfast burritos from the kitchen. And until recently, access to the produce section was actually blocked by the checkout line. Shoppers had to move through the checkout line, select their produce, then return through the lane to the back of the line—a troublesome detour even when customers were not in line, much less when they were.

The Sacaton market, like other minimarkets on the reservation, may be convenient but is not considered by anyone (except, perhaps, kids) to be the ideal source for most of a family's groceries. For this, someone must travel. The shopper drives (or gets a ride) to a nearby town and one of several grocery chains—there is a variety around the perimeter of the reservation. In fact, if I had to identify a fourth focal point of life on the reservation, it would be transportation.

My experience of life at Gila River has been characterized by most of the same concerns Pimas face: summertime temperatures, adequate cooling in the house, and reasonable access to good food. When the time came to move to the reservation for full-time research, my closest Pima friend was living in her parents' home with her own young son. They hadn't couch space to spare, let alone a private room where I could store equipment and work in privacy. The hospital had some housing available for rotating medical interns. I had used this housing frequently during the past three years for short stays and found it sterile but adequate. That housing also placed me in the center of Sacaton, which was exceptionally convenient. Among the residents of that housing were much-needed physicians, physical therapists, and eye doctors serving short terms in this initially exotic but ultimately somewhat boring (vis-à-vis nightlife) location. But because of the hospital's pressing need for those interns—and its relative lack of need for anthropologists—those beds were unavailable to me for any more than a few days at a time.

Bearing the same name as the dam that claimed the lower Gila River, the town of Coolidge lies less than a mile from the southeastern edge of the reservation. This poor to lower-middle-class farming community occupies the area surrounding the ruins of a major Hohokam center, Casa Grande. The archaeological significance of this area made Coolidge more attractive than either the Phoenix suburbs, north of the reservation, or the busy but also poor town of Casa Grande to the southwest. The size and pace of Coolidge were also more comparable to the reservation "capital" of Sacaton than to the other two. So this would become my home base.

Once settled in Coolidge, I could observe and participate in life at Gila River on a more constant schedule, beginning with the most mundane activities. It is a hackneyed truth that life moves slowly on the reservation. Pimas at the hospital—but also in the store and in tribal buildings and wherever I saw them—moved as if with some hidden tenderness, like stitches or childbirth contractions; others appeared slowed by grief or some other tremendous distraction. Even those with upright and cheerful faces were moving at a pace that looked purposefully halted. Luckily—that is, before I had made any inappropriate expressions of sympathy or aid—I recognized this to be a cultural difference in pace. My own fast way of moving and speaking was, to Pimas, a jarring marker of difference. Slowing took enormous personal scrutiny. For months, every first step—after taking a sip from a drinking fountain, upon disembarking from my car, whenever I got up from a seat—was comparably breakneck.

Markers of belonging?: where to get a homemade breakfast burrito, where to do my grocery shopping, what to do for birthdays and holidays, and how to express my various needs in the more polite, indirect fashion. I agonized through relationship tests involving monetary loans, rides to and from the bar (or places conspicuously near a bar), and notorious womanizers both single and married. Even the speed and routes of my driving became an indication of my familiarity with the reservation and its ways. All of these are characteristic of participant observation, the methodology of choice for anthropologists.

The Pima women I was looking for were like cicadas: easy to identify and approach but hard to pin down. Arranging introductions or meetings that would foster an equal and open interaction took years of training and preparation. There were several layers of acquaintance that preceded these friendships. Moving out from my volunteer position at the DEC, my first and most influential relationship was with a politically active and well-known Pima man who took an interest in my work, and who would make the elaborate maze of tribal offices and departments, alliances and rivalries seem approachable. At the same time, another man, who was too much of a loner to become an ally, was also taking an interest in my work. More skeptical and guarded, John (a pseudonym) asked to meet me not on the reservation but 90 minutes away in Tucson at a pancake house near the highway connecting Tucson to the reservation. Conversations with John were always steered by his burning skepticism and occasional fury at what he considered wasted money, pointless research, and failed programs for diabetes on the reservation. In fact, I consider John to be one of the Pimas' most vocal advocates for Indian rights and self-determination, ever attentive to the destructive impact of the dominant culture and capitalist relations. Yet we most times agreed about how things should be done vis-à-vis diabetes and who should be in charge of such efforts.

I continued to make friends and contacts in the community, principally by being there. The landscape of my participant observation included: hospital classes on prenatal health and diabetes education; public health clinic office-waiting-room and prenatal visits; public health field clinics; outpatient health clinics; the Mul-cha-tha (footrace) festival; several holiday parades and parties throughout the year; health walks and exercise events put on by the Fitness Center and Hu Hu Kam Hospital; cooking classes; family memorials and birthday parties; crystal and Avon parties; and countless lunches and dinners with community members.

But it took two and a half years to develop what I would call friendships with the women who were a part of or closely peripheral to the study. Once established, these friendships quickly became close, due in part to the intimacy of the research questions. By this point, unless I did something untoward, it was only after five o'clock p.m. or in particularly private settings that my presence on the reservation was conspicuous. Community bingo night, in people's homes, in the store on weekends—these are the times when locals noticed and acknowledged me, moving me into the liminal space that plenty of Anglos who work every day on the reservation never approach. After two and a half years here on a part-time basis, I was finally invited to my first family memorial, spent my first nights in Pima homes, and began in earnest to study life at Gila River.

Participant observation is daily bread to an ethnographer. Living among and as the people do gives us our best hope for understanding their ways and beliefs. This methodology demands a familiarity with one's subjects, with their language and nonverbal forms of communication, and with all aspects of their lives that can possibly be shared. Participant observation often distinguishes the anthropologist from other social scientists, and for good reason. Anthropologists typically relinquish statistical significance in favor of more detailed descriptions and explanations of important events. We attend to context and meaning, norm and idiosyncrasy, change and variation. The very questions asked by the ethnographer sometimes preclude statistical measurement. And we embrace this "limitation." Indeed, to anthropologists, participant observation frees us to ask the most important question: Why?

At the invitation of the DEC director, I first visited Sacaton to help with a study of that program's health outcomes. I describe that study in the next chapter. The director and I were particularly interested in outcomes of the education program for pregnant women. What was the impact of the classes? Did diabetes education help women keep their blood sugar level down during pregnancy? Did completion of prenatal education modules correlate with a reduction in birth defects and other neonatal problems? Why were they so important that a diabetes class was arranged just for them? How did they respond to the classes? And, I would later ask, what about all the pregnant women who never attended these classes? As I began my visits to the reservation, several times every month over the next two and a half years, the centrality of pregnant women in the diabetes epidemic began slowly to dawn on me.

Diabetes screenings and testing have been commonplace here for decades. The DEC was one of the original model programs designed by the Indian Health Service (IHS) in the 1970s to promote diabetes prevention. Pimas were assumed (and in the early 1990s shown) to have a genetic predisposition to diabetes. During the early months of my work at Gila River, I was still learning about the role of gestational diabetes in the future diabetic health of the woman and her baby. But providers at Gila River had known about it for years. The DEC had recently hired a new diabetes educator[3] specifically devoted to the management of these prenatal cases. Physicians and nurses in the prenatal clinic rightfully considered themselves part of the front line in diagnosing diabetes early. Pregnant women are a captive audience, so to speak, already targeted for and very much participating in prenatal care on the reservation. So it was not difficult to add a message about diabetes to their prenatal regimen.

Also during my early fieldwork, new research was showing the role of the intrauterine environment in diabetes. Pregnant women's experiences—in diet, exercise, and perhaps even stress—would also have an impact on the future diabetic health of their babies. This impact came not simply from the genes they passed down involuntarily but from their behaviors and experiences, influenced as they sometimes are by poverty, limited education, and childhoods around domestic violence and substance abuse. These findings would tear pregnant women from their relative anonymity among all at-risk Pimas, to the very center of prevention efforts. The impact of this focus has yet to be fully seen, but pregnant women were clearly becoming the most important group to watch.

My research goal became clear. I wanted to understand the real context of pregnancy on this reservation and what it meant for this intergenerational diabetes epidemic. If diabetes was passed down not just genetically but through behavioral mechanisms, what caused those behaviors? How did Pimas view this disease? Did they understand biomedical ideas about how it was passed on? Were Pimas motivated to prevent it? Was prevention really possible or practical, given the realities of reservation life? And what stake in all of this prevention work did pregnant Pima women have? Did Pima women hold some key that would explain the high prevalence, the still high incidence, the passing down of this disease? If they did, how could I get them to talk to me about it when more than thirty-six years of researchers had already been here trying?

Participant observation was key but not enough to answer all of these questions. The second major strategy would be formal interviews. I conducted 90 between 1999 and 2000. Sixty-three of these participants agreed to be tape-recorded. Twenty-seven were pregnant women who provided up to three interviews over the course of their pregnancies; this represents 14 percent of the estimated number of women pregnant during a 10-month period.

The formal interviews—ones scheduled around a list of open-ended questions and lasting up to three hours—addressed a range of issues: Pima health knowledge, understanding of diabetes, and health-care-seeking behaviors. I began interviews with very general questions about health and illness, signs and symptoms, only later moving into diabetes. We explored ideas about disease etiology, diagnosis, comorbid conditions, prevention, education, the social implications of disease, and treatment. I was, as any anthropologist would be, careful to use culturally relevant, nonjargon terms and tried to encourage women's openness and reflection. I was also careful not to insinuate any clinical expertise or affiliation (or allegiance) to the hospital. This, for two reasons: first, many previous research projects in the community offered diagnostic and treatment services to participants, which I clearly could not offer; second, most of the non-Indians on the reservation did indeed work for the Health Care Corporation, so it was reasonable to try to distinguish myself from them.

Recruiting people for interviews was a carefully scripted, although deceptively simple, activity. I stationed myself at offices, clinics, and events that attracted Pima women,[4] giving out flyers that described the research and its approval by the tribal council and Health Care Corporation, and which listed my home phone number. In these settings, my presence was clearly out of the ordinary. Some women might have thought I had Indian heritage and was availing myself of the IHS services, free to all tribal members nationwide. At the moment after women had settled in for their wait, I quietly and succinctly introduced myself and offered them a flyer. In about two sentences, I tried to state the reason for the research, what their role in it would be, the amount of compensation, and that it would occur at their home or away from the clinic or office. Most women expressed their interest in the topic and scheduled the interview right then. Then came the complicated business of drawing an accurate map to their home. Women who were not interested also declined right away. There was never any euphemistic small talk or promise to call later. It was either yes or no.

The majority of the interviews (75 percent) occurred in the woman's home. We sat in the living room, kitchen, back yard, or desert behind her house, wherever she felt most comfortable. I feared, due to the length of the interviews and some rumors of negative sentiments about research, that participation rates would be low. On the contrary, women seemed eager to talk.

The reservation is divided into seven districts for purposes of representation and resource allocation. These districts are not uniform in size or population, nor are they very similar. Each has a slightly different character, due to subtle differences in landscape, population density, and availability of services. It was important to me, and particularly to the tribal council members, that I talk to several people in every district. A table in Appendix B shows the distribution of participants according to the district in which they lived. The population centers (districts 3 and 6) were most heavily represented in the sample due largely to the fact that women from these districts have the easiest access to the hospital and clinic where recruitment was done. But I also conducted focus groups in districts 2, 5, and 7 to help increase my sample from these districts. (See Appendix C for a summary of these groups.) We—that is, the tribal council and I—considered my sample reasonably broad, especially given the descriptive—rather than statistical—purpose of my work.

These interviews would be critical. As a research method, lengthy interviews are a fairly novel approach at Gila River. And this novelty was popular. If nothing else, Pima women would say, "we like to talk." And their desert homes encouraged open and unstructured conversations. They were on their own "turf." They could decide whether others were present and when to end the conversation. Conducting interviews in women's homes also facilitated participant observation of women's lives. I could observe women's interactions with family and friends—particularly how they explained the purpose of my visit. I could see how they spent their time, even observe what they ate. Overall, participant observation and local interviews were methods that transformed this research into something meaningful, far more than could have been achieved in the hospital.

These settings were, however, not always the best for making tape recordings. Wind, traffic, playing children, or television sets being watched by others in the room created significant amounts of noise during many of the interviews. Despite attempts with three different microphones, a few recorded interviews were inaudible and could not be transcribed. Quotes from these women are not available, although their demographic data and responses to questions were recorded in field notes. It is unfortunate to lose even a single recording, but this cost is preferable to insisting on an impossible quiet or privacy.

Most Pimas are reluctant to "preach" or speak in an authoritative voice on topics as complex as diabetes. Question them about "norms," and you elicit blank stares and grunts of hesitation. Ask them what "should" occur, and get an awkward silence. But ask Pimas to talk about what they and friends have experienced, and answers are free-flowing, often opinionated, and elaborated with stories and emotion. Through their stories, women produced metanarratives about their own and others' behaviors. So where aloof, objective questioning got little response, a bit of social time in women's home environments put them at ease and facilitated the discussion of cultural ideals in an indirect way.

Another rule I carefully observed—a rule related to the slower pace on the reservation—was to wait patiently for answers. Women often elaborated their answers, but only after what seemed a long silence. If I used multiple forms of a question, I got women's responses for each, so that I could determine which form worked best. For example, I asked all women, "Do you think you'll get diabetes?" and waited for their response before posing a similar question, "Do you think diabetes is unavoidable?" These questions elicit entirely different responses on more than one topic, including one's sense of personal defense or resilience against diabetes; avoidability for an individual versus Pima society in general; and information about how "typical" one considers oneself of all Pimas. Multiple versions of the same question often helped parse out the individual's view of herself vis-à-vis Pima society in general. That is, by probing more deeply through similar questions, I got women to talk about how their experience and behaviors might have been normal or atypical for Gila River.

These critical interviews, then, became conversations. As we wove through topics of health, experience of health care and illness, and pregnancy, our conversations opened a window onto the common yet largely obscure experience of diabetes in this community. Despite decades of research on the topic here, Pimas remain reactive, reflective, and very private about this disease. Most of these women grew up in the context of endemic disease. Pregnant women's perspectives did not have the sense of urgency or trauma that might be associated with other prenatal diseases. Theirs is a seasoned view of diabetes and its impact, not simply on individual lives but on the life and identity of the community.

My methods have some predictable strengths: the strength of participant observation, of lengthy open-ended interviews in women's homes, of several years' work on the community before beginning formal interviews, of being female and within fifteen years of age of most of my informants. But the biggest weakness and the one I am inclined to address at the outset is my neglect of men's perspectives. By piggybacking on prenatal health care as a source for informants and a major topic of discussion, I necessarily perpetuate some patterns of that system, namely, an absence of most fathers. Gender inequities in health care are significant. The exposure of sexism in biomedical ideologies is clearly relevant to this work. But while I reference much of that work here, I have not made it the fulcrum of my analysis.

My principal goal was to counterbalance the impact of medical and genetic statistics on the Pima. Statistics generalize. Narratives, on the other hand, elaborate. I tried to locate individual lives and self-perceptions of diabetes and was increasingly drawn to pregnancy as a real and symbolic starting point for this disease. My goals required a nearness and constancy over time to my sources and led to that signature approach of anthropology, participant observation. I daresay I took participant observation just a little more seriously than some. I sought common ground with Pima women, not in gender or age alone, but in my own first experience of pregnancy as it unfolded simultaneously with these women's. I participant-observed pregnancy.

3

Why Prenatal Diabetes?

"Why aren't you talking about all Pima diabetes?" One tribal council member, who is acutely aware that diabetes kills Pimas at four times the rate for white Americans, questioned me about the narrow focus of my study. Prenatal diabetes or gestational diabetes mellitus (GDM), the relatively unknown version of this disease, is largely invisible to both the afflicted and the rest of Pima society. The really notorious co-morbidities of diabetes—amputations, dialysis, blindness—are characteristic not of pregnancies but of more aged populations; so why target a prenatal pathology if mothers are symptomless and the elevated blood sugar vanishes at birth?

The proper answer to the councilman's question—why prenatal diabetes?—is not alone that gestational diabetes and its immediate effects—increased likelihood for cesarean, maternal hypertensive disorders, high infant birth weight and glucose levels, birth trauma, and even fetal death—are well worth suppressing in themselves. More to the point of "all Pima diabetes," GDM afflicts both mothers and fetuses with a greater susceptibility to later-life diabetes: excessive blood sugar in utero adds a new biological insult to the Pimas' embedded genetic predisposition to diabetes, and so delivers to both mother and fetus a potent dose of increased risk that does not recede at birth with the evidence of its presence.

The intergenerational impact of the womb environment also accumulates in each generation. Imagine now a scenario (that will be demonstrated in chapter 8) in which six or seven generations ago the Pima nation experienced a severe famine. Malnourished fetuses developed slight defects in the way their bodies metabolize glucose—"defects" that might have been adaptive changes in other circumstances. In their own lifetimes, those children experienced not another famine but a feast of fat and glucose, which their impaired systems cautiously, frugally stored up for future use. Their own children continued the store-housing of that excess, and so developed hyperinsulinemia, insulin resistance, and by adulthood, glucose intolerance. That scenario of accumulating and aggravating diabetic tendencies, if allowed to continue, might eventually accelerate the rate and onset of diabetes until teenagers (and thus all pregnant women) would commonly have outright diabetes, or, hypothetically, until many babies are born in diabetic distress.

Research has confirmed the possibility of this scenario through a greater transmission of diabetes from mothers than from fathers (Dorner and Mohnike 1976), from mothers who had diabetes during pregnancy than from mothers who were not diabetic during pregnancy (Pettitt et al. 1988; Pettitt et al. 1996), and in detailing the effect of a diabetic environment in utero on predisposition to type 2 diabetes (Sobngwi et al. 2003). In sum, both a mother's genes and her behaviors potentiate diabetes; an impact that carries over into her children and grandchildren.

My answer to the councilman's question was, therefore, that I was (and am) "talking about all Pima diabetes" when I insist that GDM preys insidiously on Pima babies, generation after generation. Combating GDM effectively is the linchpin of a coherent strategy against Pima diabetes in all its manifestations. This is the operating premise of the tribe's Diabetes Education Center (DEC), which aims to ameliorate the biological components of diabetes inheritance—namely, the toxic intrauterine environment—so that the fetus's genetic predisposition to diabetes is not exacerbated.

But is this the best approach? While prenatal health care is known to improve birth outcome, its utilization by women has been shown to correlate with various demographic, social, economic, and psychological factors (Lazarus 1990; Lazarus 1997; Oropesa et al. 2000). Rich ethnographic data illuminate the barriers to prenatal care, particularly for minority groups, in a variety of settings (e.g., Browner and Sargent 1996; Celik and Hotchkiss 2000; Gertler et al. 1993; Lewando-Hundt et al. 2001; Lia-Hoagberg et al. 1990; Raghupathy 1996; Sargent and Rawlins 1991). So it could not be assumed that pregnant Pima women were (a) getting and (b) benefiting from diabetes education.

In 1997, the DEC director did not know definitively whether education was helping pregnant Pima women, and she advertised for help to conduct a study of just that. For that study, I would measure the relationship between diabetes education and maternal glucose control during pregnancy. Prenatal diabetes education is designed to help women understand diabetes and its complications during pregnancy, to teach self–blood glucose monitoring (SBGM), and, when needed, to ensure that women have and understand their medications. Not surprisingly, increased patient knowledge is supposed to improve the likelihood that women achieve and maintain good blood glucose control (Dunn et al. 1990).

A common measure of a person's glucose control is the hemoglobin A1c ("A1c" hereafter), a blood measure that reports the average amount of sugar in the blood over the past three months. When sugar in the bloodstream attaches to the hemoglobin in red blood cells (a process called glycosylation), it remains for the life of the cell, or about 120 days. The more sugar in the bloodstream, the more sugar will be attached to the red blood cells. The A1c expresses blood sugar as a percent and reflects a weighted average of a person's blood sugar over the previous three to four months (Franz 2001). Three to four months of intervention (education, case management) is, therefore, long enough for women to positively impact this cumulative measure of their blood glucose. It is not so long, however, that behavioral and dietary changes made just for the prenatal period would be missed. The A1c test was therefore the preferred measure of maternal health outcome. For pregnant Pima women, an A1c of less than 0.06 mmol/l is considered "in control."

Diabetic women are referred to the DEC at the first recognition of pregnancy. All others undergo periodic tests during pregnancy to watch for the first discernible signs of the disease. Once enrolled in the DEC, all women receive education, case management, blood glucose monitoring supplies, referrals, and support for maintaining good blood sugar control. The prenatal diabetes education program includes 16 learner objectives (see table 3.1), taught over the course of the pregnancy and covering nutrition, exercise, psychosocial health and adjustment, basic education on diabetes etiology and complications, self-monitoring of blood glucose, and a separate objective dedicated to complications specific to diabetes during pregnancy. These objectives are reached with the aid of videos, worksheets, pamphlets, and models including plastic foods, for example, to demonstrate appropriate portions.

Table 3.1 Diabetes education learner objectives

Topic	Objectives
Nutrition	1. Participant states two healthy eating changes specifically for pregnancy to keep blood sugar in control
	2. Participant identifies the three foods/beverages that are empty calories and raise blood sugar
	3. Participant identifies the three food groups that provide carbohydrates and predominantly regulate blood sugar
Exercise	4. Participant describes a safe exercise plan for herself stating type, duration, and frequency
	5. Participant lists three guidelines to follow for a safe exercise program
Psychosocial	6. Participant describes her feelings about diagnosis of diabetes and feelings about pregnancy
	7. Participant describes her responsibility in care and how to use resources in the community to meet care needs
Understanding	8. Participant describes what gestational diabetes is and how it differs from pregestational diabetes
	9. Participant states blood-sugar goals for pregnancy
Monitoring	10. Participant explains procedure for monitoring fetal movement and why it is done
	11. Participant lists three things she can do to control her blood sugar during pregnancy
	12. Participant describes her plans for diabetes prevention/control after delivery
	13. Participant describes one thing/situation that hinders her progress toward achieving her behavior change goals
	14. Participant demonstrates correct procedure for self–blood glucose monitoring during pregnancy
Complications	15. Participant lists two complications for baby if blood sugar is high during pregnancy
	16. Participant lists two complications for mother if blood sugar is high during pregnancy

The DEC staff assesses women's comprehension of education material immediately after instruction (i.e., within the same appointment). To fully meet the learning objective, women must verbalize their understanding of the concepts by identifying major points from the lesson. When appropriate, women will prove their understanding and skills through demonstration of the task (e.g., blood glucose monitoring). Whenever a woman cannot perform these tests of knowledge, the information is simply reinforced and repeated until she can. After completing the learning objectives, the pregnant woman then sets her two self-care goals. One goal is exercise-oriented, the other is a dietary change or a new self-care behavior such as SBGM. DEC staff track women's progress toward these goals during the postpartum period.

To analyze the effectiveness of prenatal diabetes education, I used a random 33 percent sample (n = 146) of all women identified by the DEC as having a pregnancy and either gestational or "outright" diabetes between 1994 and 2001.[1] The women's hospital records were excavated for data on maternal glucose control, education completion, and delivery type (vaginal or C-section), as well as cases of fetal demise (table 3.2). Infant charts were reviewed also, although only Hu Hu Kam Memorial Hospital charts were used. Births do not occur at this hospital, so if infants were never seen at Hu Hu Kam Memorial Hospital, birth information was obtained from the mother's chart. I also collected information about the program's history, procedures, and practices during monthly meetings with DEC staff. These meetings included many one-on-one discussions with DEC educators and directors, as well as the progress reports I gave periodically to the gathered DEC staff.

The DEC estimated there to be between 250 and 300 pregnancies per year at Gila River, and that approximately 50 of these are diagnosed diabetic pregnancies. The DEC claimed to reach 85 to 95 percent of diabetic pregnancies (40 to 50 each year, plus about 20 women who had impaired glucose tolerance [IGT]) because a good network of communication exists between the several providers in contact with pregnant women. Pima women might also have information on the whereabouts and health of friends and family, and that information is expertly captured by some of the longer-term DEC employees.

However, there was a good deal of fluctuation in annual program enrollment: from 50 in 1994, to 75 in years 1995–1998, to around 30 in years 1999–2001. Since no reduction in the rates of pregnancy or of gestational diabetes was expected in those years, the DEC staff

Table 3.2 Delivery and birth information from hospital record review

Hospital information	1994	1995	1996	1997	1998	1999	2000	2001
Number of charts reviewed (33% of enrolled women)	17	25	25	24	24	9	12	10
Pregnancies ending in fetal demise	2	2	2	2	5	1	0	0
C-section delivery	3	3	4	6	4	7	3	4
Other information								
Miscarriage/fetal demise	2	3	3	1	5	1	0	0
Cesarean delivery	2	4	4	6	5	5	3	4
Congenital malformation	2	3	1	2	0	0	4	2
Other perinatal morbidity/mortality	5	5	6	10	7	7	5	2
High birth weight	4	2	3	2	4	1	5	2
Low birth weight	0	0	2	3	—	—	—	—

suggested employee turnover as a causal factor for the variation. I say more about this issue in the next chapter.

The Nutrition Objective is typically the first to be completed by women entering the DEC and is the objective most women complete each year (table 3.3). The average gestation of women's pregnancies at enrollment is 11.24 weeks. Since congenital malformations are largely determined by diet and other factors during the first eight weeks of pregnancy (Kitzmiller et al. 1996; Mills et al. 1979), education efforts with first-time mothers do not have an impact on these malformations.[2] However, mothers completing education may benefit in future pregnancies by education received and preconceptual counseling on the risks of high maternal blood glucose in early pregnancy (Charron-Prochownik 2000).

These statistics offer important information about the education services. But to know if education was doing any good, I had to discover a statistically significant correlation between education and ma-

Table 3.3 Percentage of women completing learning objectives by year

Topic	1994 (%)	1995 (%)	1996 (%)	1997 (%)	1998 (%)	1999 (%)	2000 (%)	2001 (%)
Nutrition	82	92	88	78	79	22	75	60
Fitness	29	36	64	67	38	67	67	50
Psychosocial	6	24	48	50	29	33	67	70
Understanding	18	28	72	58	42	56	75	70
Monitoring	12	32	72	58	63	56	67	30
Complications	6	28	60	54	33	67	67	50

ternal glucose control. For that correlation, I tested two different variables for their relationship to the completion of education objectives: the last A1c for each mother before childbirth, which (I presumed) would show her "best" or lowest blood glucose level, and the percentage of all A1c levels taken that were in control or less than 0.06 mmol/l, which might show a degree or measure of control across the pregnancy (table 3.4). Only the last A1c model produced a significant overall p-value ($p = .000$) when regressed against objective completion rates. The R-squared values for each model (.226 for the last A1c model, .055 for the percentage in control model) showed that the last A1c model explains a greater percentage of variation within the sample. That is, the last A1c model explained 23 percent of the variation, while the percentage in control model explained only 6 percent of the variation. The last A1c model was, therefore, chosen for use in evaluating its relationship to education completion rates.

Using the last maternal A1c value as the dependent variable, I then performed a multiple regression and Pearson correlation against all six education topics. Two education objectives showed a significant correlation: the Fitness Objective and the Complications Objective. Pearson correlations also show that the Fitness Objective and Complications Objective were the best predictors of a reduction in maternal A1c, although all of them had a slight positive impact. Taking the regression and Pearson correlation data together suggests there is a relationship between completion of learning objectives and maternal glucose control. So while the education services are very beneficial, women are not reached early enough in pregnancy and are not always completing the program once enrolled.

Table 3.4 Multiple regression and Pearson coefficients for learning objectives and last A1c

Topic	p-value	t-value	P (two-tail)	Pearson coefficient to last A1c
Nutrition	.440	−0.282	0.778	−0.230
Fitness	.078	−2.248	0.026	−0.401
Psychosocial	.228	−0.670	0.504	−0.355
Understanding	.098	1.000	0.319	−0.317
Monitoring	.125	−0.841	0.402	−0.362
Complications	.005	−2.146	0.034	−0.419

These correlations raise further questions about the usefulness of the other four topics for achieving A1c levels in control. No statistically significant relationship exists between the timing of education and maternal glucose control, although this may have been attributable in part to sample size. Several other confounding factors are possible. Women who are able to attend classes also have better access to transportation for all health care appointments. Those same women might also be more "compliant" with healthcare in general than women who would not attend DEC classes. Participation in the classes may serve a reminding or social support function that correlates with improved prenatal care (fig. 3.1). So women who do not attend classes, even if they obtain education and knowledge through some other means, would not have this social support or helpful reminders. If this "self-selection" bias is in place, then the most difficult cases of diabetes to prevent and treat will be among people who drop out of treatment or never complete a referral to the DEC.

The outcome study results offered helpful information to DEC staff about internal performance (e.g., the documentation of appointments and education objectives covered) and about the comparative influence of each topic on maternal A1c control, but little about the reasons women participated or failed to participate in diabetes education. Since only 23 percent of the variation in women's glucose control was explained by education, the inscrutability of other factors influencing women's glucose control is of great consequence.

My ethnographic work, inspired by these outcome data and their limitations, cast a broader net. Women who were not enrolled in diabetes education were my principal target. The factors that kept them from care—logistical, cultural, or other—were my principal concern.

Figure 3.1. A mother and child attending a focus group on prenatal diabetes. The low-fat sandwich was part of a provided lunch, while the juice came from home. This mother-child dyad, and the food shared between mothers and children both before and after birth, may be the key to reversing the diabetes epidemic.

The success of this intervention program—indeed, the etiology behind Sara's comment, "It's just how Pimas are"—has moved beyond important and is now critical. I argue in the coming chapters, much as I did at my tribal council review, that pregnant women will be central in the effort to stem Pima diabetes. The tribal council did not that day adopt my confidence in GDM as the linchpin of Pima diabetes, but they did not reject it. As my interviews progressed, the tribal council would begin to see pregnant women not necessarily for their role in the intergenerational chain of diabetes, but as influential and knowledgeable spokespersons for the Pima experience of this disease and its treatment. What the tribal council wisely noted was that these were narratives of Pimas typically missed by prevention campaigns. These women, speaking in the privacy of their homes, tell why the diabetes epidemic goes unchecked.

Part II

4

Obstacles to Treatment

As I began this ethnographic research, I noticed the same faces regularly at DEC appointments and classes. I also knew about the many DNKAs ("dinkas" or "Did Not Keep Appointment" in the ubiquitous acronyms of technological culture) that dotted the appointment books at the DEC, the prenatal clinic, and other departments. Why were not all Pimas seen regularly at the hospital, well in advance of any signs of diabetes, eager for prevention education and advice? Why didn't more, if not all, Pimas respond immediately and fully to advice offered? These questions could be applied to millions of Americans who don't adhere to a healthy regimen of low-fat, high-fruit and vegetable diets. Further, nonattendance of diabetes care appointments is a problem across all ethnic, age, and health sectors (Beckles et al. 1998; Broussard et al. 1982; Narayan et al. 1998). So a categorization of Pimas' reactions to health care proved to be not so different from any patient group across the nation.

My first guess for explaining this phenomenon was that patients could be categorized into one of two categories: (1) "biomedically friendly" patients who generally follow instructions because of their respect for or belief in biomedical care, and (2) patients who generally disagree with or are "noncompliant" with biomedical care and/or its practitioners. Such a tidy distinction, however, does not exist at Gila River, or anywhere. Instead, patients have mixed feelings about biomedical care and are compliant and noncompliant in varying degrees under different circumstances.

People with chronic diabetes have long been viewed as "preferring less active involvement" in the management of the disease (Case Management Advisor 2002; Wellbery 2003). But the same research showed that patients who perceived their physician as facilitating their involvement in care and decision making were more pleased with care. In other words, people with chronic conditions need their health care providers to show them how to get involved, to help them feel motivated, and to guide their energies. A clear relationship exists between a physician's encouragement of patient involvement or autonomy and the patient's ultimate satisfaction with care (Glasgow et al. 2003). Not to put too fine a point on it, some researchers have even suggested that the physician's attitude may be more important than his or her actual knowledge of the disease (Weinberger et al. 1984). So it is not so much what the providers say to these patients with chronic diseases, but how they say it. These processual factors, like motivational counseling, are not the only ones contributing to satisfaction with care. Patients report being most pleased with their diabetes health care when they also have:

- health coverage
- one doctor for diabetes care
- several provider care practices over the previous year, including examination of HbA1c, feet, eyes, cholesterol, and gums
- counseling on diet, exercise, weight control, and blood glucose management (Narayan et al. 1999)

This checklist of services (excluding health coverage) essentially matches the ADA guidelines for diabetes care. At Gila River, health coverage is available to all residents through the tribal hospital. Patients may see the same doctor for their diabetes care, although they must plan in advance and call for their appointments on specific days each month. And the provider care practices listed above are scrupulously monitored, scheduled, and rescheduled by the DEC and other providers.

But none of these care practices was a major concern for the Pima women I spoke to. Instead, their major concerns about health care had to do with time spent waiting for appointments, transportation, and confidentiality. The majority of these women follow the advice and prescriptions of their providers. But of those who expressed a criticism about the health care offered, there was some agreement that their pregnancies and their bodies were being considered out of context. Care was at the providers' convenience, not always their own, and cultural differences were affecting the encounters in subtle but important ways. The importance of context is evident in the realizations of the last two chapters, namely, that diabetes education was helping a few Pimas but left many out; that those Pimas avoiding health care were doing so for identifiable, and sometimes simple, reasons; and that these issues would not always be evident to or shared with providers.

The stories women told about their health care are, in some ways, impossible to categorize, and I will not force categories here. But they do offer windows onto the experience and perception of illness in the community. I have included stories that illustrate the most common barriers to participation in health care and diabetes prevention—wait time, transportation, and confidentiality—as well as stories that were less commonly voiced but illuminative of the context.

These were stories about how they'd been treated when they had a ruptured appendix, or their niece had bronchitis, or their cousin had been diagnosed with diabetes. What struck me was not that women had complaints about medical care, since that is hardly unique to Pimas, but that I could elicit these stores without much probing. Ignored by traditional patient questionnaires and abbreviated or forgone in rushed appointments, these are stories of women who had already expressed an overall positive feeling about health care on the reservation. These were important elaborations.

Pima women (see p. 173, note 5) typically had positive things to say about health care on the reservation. So why were there so many dinkas, and more importantly, why weren't Pimas doing more as a community to prevent diabetes? To start to better understand Pima attitudes about health, I posed the very broad question: "In general, how do you feel about the health care you receive on the reservation?" A majority of women (52 out of the 63 who gave recorded interviews) made positive comments overall about the care they receive, such as Mary, who reported her care at the hospital to be "all right" and that she didn't "have any problems with it." Priscilla spoke specifically about the DEC staff: "They're OK. They're real professional like, but still, in the same, they are friendly."

Five women singled out their own physician for praise, like this young woman with diabetes:

> **CS-M:** How do you feel about the care that you get at the hospital?
> **Angela:** Its all right. I like it. It's nice. They're nice people there. My doctor, she's nice. If you're in pain, she'll give you medicine. You just tell her what you need, and she's right there, she'll give it to you.

CS-M: And you see the same doctor every time?
Angela: Um hm. . . . Dr. Y, she's the nicest lady.

Negative comments would arise only later in the interview. Speaking in their own homes, women saw the interview as an opportunity to voice their concerns. I had ensured them of confidentiality and had promised to take their comments and recommendations to the hospital's board of directors and to the tribal council. Since I had also asked many questions on a variety of topics, women had the opportunity to elaborate on their initial responses. And many told stories.

Transportation

Prenatal care can be as far as 35 miles away for some reservation residents. There are only one hospital and one satellite clinic providing prenatal services for the 372,000-acre reservation. For the longer journeys, vehicle transportation is essential. But even for those living within a few blocks of either the clinic or hospital, the extremely high temperatures in this part of the Sonoran Desert (110–120 degrees Fahrenheit each day of the summer), make walking an impossible alternative for some and a generally unpopular one to most.

Sarah: For most of the elders around here, it's transportation. They don't know how to get transportation.

Mary: Sometimes it's hard because I don't have transportation. . . . Sometimes [I take the van service], and sometimes they don't show up and that's it. [I miss my appointment.]

Data from the 2000 U.S. Census reveal that 46.9 percent of families on the Gila River Indian Reservation lived below the poverty level and that median household income was $18,599 (U.S. Bureau of the Census 2000). Not surprisingly, a majority of women (71 percent) said they did not own a car. These data combined with observations confirm that reliable transportation to medical appointments is a significant problem for many women.

Lack of transportation is just one of many socioeconomic barriers to better health care for all of the nation's poor. And it is with these barriers that physicians become the most frustrated, as described by this physician's assistant in a recent study:

I think most of them have 10 or 15 concerns that are ahead of the diabetes, so we're having to get through all those things before we hit the behavior change in dealing with diabetes. You know, child-care issues, transportation issues, violence. Everything. You've got to find out those things that are ahead of the diabetes. (Freeman and Loewe 2000:509)

Confidentiality

Concerns about confidentiality also kept a few women away. These concerns stem primarily from the fact that many employees at the hospital are community members and know the patients or their families. In a small community, where "everybody knows everybody," spending large amounts of time in the waiting room can put a woman in an awkward situation of having to explain her presence to those she may meet there. The following quotes reveal the potential conflicts for pregnant women seeking care:

Eileen: I took the pregnancy test at the store because I was scared to go to the hospital. People over there stare.

Fay: I'd rather be home than be anywhere out there. . . . I think I'm comfortable here, I can do anything here, I can eat anything. Then like at the hospital, you know, people stare too, and I hate it because they just look at you. Like they're trying to figure out who you are.

Nancy: They stare at you, the people waiting out in the waiting room.

Standard procedures for protection of confidentiality are in place at Hu Hu Kam Memorial Hospital, including record sign-out requirements and locked storage of medical records. But while medical-records, secretarial, and clinical staff work to protect the privacy of patients, there are some unavoidable pitfalls to participating in hospital-based care, including the public nature of waiting areas. The lack of privacy in the large waiting area for the outpatient clinic is exacerbated by the familiarity of small communities, reservation or not.

For women who knew, or were known by, hospital staff, there was the added concern of staff-to-staff gossip:

Patricia: I make [appointments], then I just don't go. . . . It's OK, but the people that work there, they'll be reading about your information to other people, talk about you and stuff. That, that I don't like. Everybody knows everybody around here, and they like to talk. So they tell everything about you, even [private] things.

This narrative is anecdotal, and I did not survey women on this particular concern about confidentiality. But it does point to a problem specific to the reservation (or small town), and one which could be quite difficult to correct without the most draconian of information management rules.

Doctors in Training

Elders, more than younger women, expressed the belief that the doctors at the hospital/clinic are still in training. Laura and Alice were both unsure about the qualifications of the doctors:

> **Laura:** There's still that stigmatism [sic] that the . . . the physicians are, what was the word we used to use, the physicians are trainees but there's another word.
> **CS-M:** Interns or residents?
> **Laura:** Interns, interns, yeah, interns.

> **Alice:** I think some of them don't trust . . . the doctors. When I listen to people, what I think is that they think that the doctors they sent out here are not that good. And they think that if we went to a doctor in town [off reservation] someplace, they would know right away what's wrong with us. They would treat us for that thing.

Since the 1960s, the reservation hospital in Sacaton has hosted physician residents or interns in specific realms of medical care. Community members became aware of this program and began to attribute medical errors and poor treatment to the students. Even though the interns are only a very small proportion of the hospital staff, some community members retain some distrust or skepticism about the professional status of the hospital staff. These ideas, though erroneous, are not corrected by any hospital practices, since physician credentials are not posted in the exam rooms or hallways but in their offices, where patients are less likely to visit.

These views led a few Pimas, including some hospital employees, to seek their care off-reservation:

> **CS-M:** Is there anything that you would change about the health programs on the reservation if you could?

Gloria: Better doctors. To me, it's just like, those doctors are just training on us, using us to get their experience. We need doctors here . . . cuz a lot of these people with insurance would rather go out than come here [to the reservation hospital].
CS-M: Have you ever done that?
Gloria: Yeah.

But few Pimas have insurance and, in this way, differ from many patients who might have some alternatives within insurance networks. The belief that the reservation doctors were "training on us" was voiced only by women who had had bad experiences or misdiagnoses during care. It is believed by women such as Gloria that doctors working off-reservation have higher qualifications and therefore make fewer mistakes.

Florence: Well, I pay for medical care because I have Blue Cross/Blue Shield for my kids. Only because . . . it's really scary. There are so many incidents that happen [of poor or harmful treatment] that I just sometimes don't trust them. How do you know, if something serious happens? I can trust them for a cold or for something minor, but not anything major. It's really scary because we don't really have the doctors that we'd really like, I mean real good doctors. Not that, I'm not saying they're bad, but I think they because the federal government has run it for so long that they can only pay them what the government rates are. So for that reason, since I started working [for the tribe], I put my kids on my insurance.

Other concerns about physician competency typically arose out of a slow or incorrect diagnosis.

Sarah: For myself everything is OK, but my daughter had a bad experience there [at the reservation hospital]. She had a gallstone, and we took her in about four or three o'clock in the morning. And she stayed there until about eight o'clock before they finally told me what it was. They were examining her, and they lifted her up off of the examining table, and . . . she was in pain after that. . . . I have, up to this day, I have no idea why they [lifted her up like] that. . . . She was just a little girl. Then to wait there all that time, and she got infected. Finally at eight o'clock, they sent us to Phoenix, and then she had emergency surgery. . . .
CS-M: Do you think that bad experience affected how you feel about going in for treatment?

Sarah: Yeah, I tried to kill myself! . . . I have to be dying, and that way they'll see me.

Sarah thought her daughter's doctor was incompetent and careless, diagnosing the gallstone problem too slowly and examining her in a way that caused her pain and, perhaps, further injury. Sarah's is also an example of an account about family members—rather than one's "own" experience—that impacts a decision to seek care or avoid care oneself.

And yet Pimas' perceptions that hospital staff have poor diagnostic skills, or that you "have to be dying" before you can be seen, are juxtaposed against providers' simultaneous opinions that Pimas "wait far too long" to come in to the hospital.

One condition was especially likely to provoke these conflicting perceptions. A fallen fontanel is a condition that is often related to dehydration in infants and is familiar to most mothers on the reservation. The area of the infant's head that feels "soft" because the skull has not closed in that spot sinks in slightly. Patricia's account tells about several things: how information is shared among family members, including appraisals of the quality of care; a folk healing practice and the ignorance of biomedical staff to this practice; and the problem-solving strategies of mothers as they use both traditional and biomedical resources for their children.

Patricia: If they're gonna help with a split-open head, you know, take them [to the hospital]. But if it's a sickness that no sign, you don't know what's going on, there's certain signs you watch for, you know certain things. Like my son, he got real sick. He wasn't eating for a couple of days. He was sleeping, he was crying, [had] the runs real bad. I mean, diaper change 10 times a day. And he wouldn't eat, wouldn't drink, sleeping, weak. . . . His head was in [fallen fontanel]. I was like, call my uncle. He pushed it up, you know. He [the baby] should have been OK. But it was the same old thing. I took him [to the hospital] and then asked the doctor. He's all, "Well, just give him Gatorade." And it made it worse. So my aunt's all, "I can't believe he told you that!" So there's some doctors that I see, they seem like they don't really know what they're doing. . . . So sometimes I don't like to take my kids to the hospital unless they really need to go.

Patricia's experience with having a family member "push up" the roof of the infant's mouth to ameliorate the fallen fontanel was not uncommon. One other mother had relatives with this skill, and it surprised them both to learn that medical doctors did not know or use this technique. That the treatment Patricia's uncle offered had failed was an indication of a more serious condition. Gatorade and other hydrating treatments were therefore viewed as ineffective and as ignoring the cause of the vomiting.

Complaints about health care should not come as a surprise in this chronically disappointed patient population. The attending doctors have a few of their own unflattering assessments of the Pima, which I discuss in chapter 6. Intuitively, one senses that these complaints and diminished expectations are not a coincidence, but rather reflect the discouraging environment in which mothers and their babies are still regularly visited by the elusive Hohokam predator.

Long Waits

The long waits were the most frequent topic of complaint.

Sherry: Oh, they take forever.

Sara: I think it's pretty good, you just need more doctors. The wait's too long.

Almost every woman either complained about wait time or knew of others who had endured unreasonable waits at the hospital or clinic. This scheduling difficulty is related to the fact that Pimas, like many Native Americans, tend to avoid confrontation or showy, attention-attracting actions. One thing I observed repeatedly was a reluctance among Pimas to complain to or remind receptionists about the length of their wait. Sarah complained that her sister waits for appointments even when she arrives on time:

Sarah: My sister kind of lives in and out of the hospital. Her appointments, she would be early and she'll just sit in there half of the afternoon.

I confirmed this to be a problem in my own visits to the hospital waiting room for recruitment and with women for appointments. The delays were largely eliminated for prenatal appointments when these services were moved into a building separate from other outpatient services. Women periodically complained about their wait times in the new building, but the waits were shorter and due to specific and more rare events (e.g., doctor's illness). The more typical, long waits in the outpatient department were due to the high number of "walk-in" patients each day. The prenatal clinic received only an occasional "walk-in" and was therefore better able to see appointments on time. Women rarely complained about wait time in the DEC, although occasional staffing shortages may be compensated for by drops in enrollment (as discussed earlier).

More recently, the hospital has instituted an appointment-booking procedure that requires patients to call on one of two days per month to schedule time with their doctor. If they miss these phone-in days, they can vie for one of a few weekday walk-in appointments on a first-come-first-served basis. This new policy is a good example of the hospital's good intentions. Intended to make it easier for patients to book appointments with their favorite provider, it also demands that they plan several days in advance just to make the appointment, and then to remember the appointment.

What we have to remember is that this hospital, like all, is in the hospitaling business. Procedures are constructed around existing assumptions that situate care on the hospital premises and relegate most health issues outside of the industrial workday (i.e., eight o'clock a.m. to five o'clock p.m.) to the Emergency Department. The bulk of the hospital resources are dedicated to patients who will present themselves for care.

An alternative vision of care would be more capable of meeting all potential patients "where they live": out in the community if not literally in their homes. While a few clinicians and public health professionals sign on for these jobs, they are not a major feature of biomedical establishments in the United States. So those Pimas who will not or cannot conform to these institutional expectations often go without care—and very often go without preventive medicine.

Knowing When to Go In

From this collection of women's stories comes not just a list of indictments against health care, for these issues are neither unique to Gila River nor even ubiquitous at Gila River. Instead, from these stories comes a clear view of Gila River women's strong sense of personal competency. For them, satisfaction with health care was a matter of self-determination, knowing when and when not to go in, and when to take or ignore medical advice:

Sara: For some things, [medicine] you know, it's just ain't gonna cure it, you know. You just need to stay home and take care of it, and medicine ain't gonna.

Sara's strong sense of personal competency in health matters is not uncommon. For example, Denise felt that medication prescriptions could and should be taken more cautiously than prescribed.

Denise: I've disagreed with the doctor, before. I'm like [thinking], I'm not gonna take your medicine or whatever I shouldn't be taking. It might do something to my body. . . .

In Denise's case, she did not speak with the provider about her concerns. Providers' advice on medications was, for both of these women, simply advice and did not carry the weight of dictum as it might among some unquestioning patients. Further, it was neither desirable nor likely that a woman would discuss these issues. A doctor prescribed what she or he thought best, and it was up to the woman to follow or reject that prescription. As in Denise's case, an outright disagreement can be upsetting and lead to future avoidance of care altogether.

Sometimes, women have specific concerns and reasons for not wanting medications or care that are not specific to Pimas, but would be quite recognizable to providers. But because of poor communication between providers and Pima women patients, these issues are not effectively managed.[1] Sherry, who works full-time for the tribe, was not attending regular appointments for supervision of her insulin therapy.

Sherry: There was some stupid reasons why I wasn't taking my diabetes [medicine]. I'm not the only one in that situation, see. When I became diabetic I lost a lot of weight. I lost, like, 113 pounds and it was just because I wasn't controlling myself but losing all that weight. I didn't want to gain it back. Then I thought, once I start taking insulin, it's gonna come back, it's gonna be awful. So for that reason, I wasn't taking my medicine.

Ethel also had concerns about her medication during pregnancy that were not allayed by her physician.

Ethel: I take the—what do you call them—depression medicine, I was taking stuff to help me go to sleep. But, to me, I don't think it helps, because I still get real depressed. And then like how they say, then I was scared because if they make it stronger, I'm scared for the baby, so I won't take them. So I kinda get scared of taking pills.

Their personal sense of being knowledgeable and competent allowed these women to manage (adjust, decline) their medications according to all of life's circumstances, rather than just the few that were discussed with the doctor.

This sense of personal competency also motivated their decisions to attend or not attend scheduled appointments. Nonattenders (or "dinkas") are a major concern of most clinics, not only for the economic cost of gaps in the appointment schedule but for the cost in terms of morbidity to those patients not maintaining a treatment regimen. Pima nonattendance is just a symptom of a much broader problem (Hardy et al. 2001). All of the concerns expressed by women —long waits, transportation, confidentiality, as well as ideas about risk and the unavoidability of disease (discussed in the last chapter)— contribute to dinkas. And Pimas are not alone in these concerns. The reasons for nonattendance cited by patients recently surveyed in the Netherlands (Spikmans et al. 2003) matched many of the concerns of Pima women:

- Lower perception of the health risks related to diabetes. I address this aspect of Pima women's narratives in detail in the next chapter, but the notion of risk is a problematic one generally, and is not evenly perceived or interpreted across different groups.
- Higher perception of difficulties related to keeping the appointment. Transportation was a dominant theme in Pima narratives, as was child care. It is not unrelated that lower socioeconomic-status patients have greater difficulty maintaining treatment regimens for all chronic diseases, not just diabetes.
- Lower perception of an ability to influence their health in general, and their diabetes in particular. I also discuss this point more fully in the next chapter and throughout the book. If diabetes is perceived as unavoidable, either because it is genetic or because the behavioral changes necessary to avoid it are too daunting, then patients tend to reduce their efforts at stemming its effects.

Strategies for improving attendance must, therefore, include improved provider/patient communication, removal or lowering of barriers produced by socioeconomic circumstances, and motivational or self-efficacy work.

Cultural Competency

The bulk of this chapter is devoted to Pima narratives about health care that are little different from what might be heard in the general population. Concerns about waiting time, socioeconomic barriers such as a lack of transportation, and confidentiality are, to varying degrees, present in health care institutions across the country. Even cultural competency, though specific in this instance to Pima culture, is an increasing concern among health care providers around the United States. These narratives too, then, tend to express feelings that many patients on reservations, in ethnic minorities, and in any cross-cultural clinical encounter might feel.

> **CS-M:** Why do you think some Pimas don't like going to the doctor?
> **Cecelia:** I think because it's the attitude of the doctor from the past, and it just reflects on them [is remembered by them]. . . . They just don't want to see them. . . . I think it's mostly non-Indian [caregivers], because they don't understand the culture. And I think with their own culture, I mean their own race, they're more open. But with the different race, it's all the difference in culture, and they just, I don't know, it just doesn't mix.

New non-Indian employees at Gila Rivers' Hu Hu Kam Memorial Hospital undergo a two-day orientation that includes just one hour of cultural and historic information on Pima farming, language, and spirituality. New employees are also driven—tourist style—around parts of the reservation where they can gaze from an air-conditioned van at the Bureau of Indian Affairs (BIA) and "sandwich" (mud) houses, a section of the Gila River Farms, one or two churches, and the Cultural Center. At the Cultural Center, they can eat a typical lunch of "Indian tacos" and tea. From this tour and the hour-long talk conducted by a community leader or elder, non-Indian providers are assumed to gain understanding of these people and their culture adequate to conduct care with respect and sensitivity. If they are not doing so, it is more likely from ignorance than from "racism," but this is not the perception of many Pimas.

One cautionary tale comes from an interaction I had with a doctor at the hospital, and helps me understand Pima perceptions of cultural ignorance on the part of hospital staff. While recruiting women for interviews, I was seated in the outpatient department and had opportunity to chat briefly with one of the doctors. He was a young and mild-mannered physician, patient and attentive in his interactions with patients. He was certainly spoken well of by staff and by the few Pima women who'd commented on their care from him. Examining the recruitment flyer on which was printed "Akimel O'odham," Dr. Z asked, "Who's this, the Akimel O'odham? These are the Tohono O'odham here, right?" The Tohono O'odham—"cousins" of the Pima—have reservations to the south and west. Dr. Z's error was not necessarily offensive, and certainly did little to affect his care of patients, but after six months' work in the community, he hadn't been taught (by the hospital orientation), told (by colleagues), or otherwise learned (from conversations with patients) the tribal name for his own patient population. If this basic information was not crossing cultural boundaries, what could providers—especially those in their first months and years of service—be expected to know about the Pima way of life?

The cultural differences between hospital staff and elder patients are most distinct, causing Sara to comment on their behalf:

> **Sara:** Some [staff] don't understand what elders have been through, or they can't always get a ride to the hospital, you know. And they get mad if you don't make the appointments, or if they finally come in for a walk-in [they say], "You haven't come at your scheduled time." I've heard people do that to elders.

It was also the elders who were less acculturated to Anglo and biomedical ways of speaking and behaving. After a long story about the death of her mother resulting from inadequate care of her asthma, Fay summarized her feelings this way:

> **Fay:** That's the sad part about some hospitals on the reservation [sic]; there is only one hospital on the reservation]. Some don't get the care they need. And it's not only like certain people that do that. I think most of the people in the hospitals do that. And it's sad . . . because some of them get treated bad. I guess it's kind of like discrimination.

So this is one collection of stories. Another collection, acquired under different circumstances and in response to different questions, might have revealed an entirely different view of health care at Gila River. Why these stories are noteworthy is that, while they mirror the same concerns of patients with and at risk for diabetes around the world, Pima women cannot be categorized as either "biomedically friendly" or "noncompliant." They have many approaches to biomedical care and have learned how to communicate and negotiate both within and outside of that "world." Pima mothers, like many women, are adept at getting biomedical care, advice, and medications when they think these are necessary, but they do not feel obligated to conform to prescription instructions or treatment plans exclusively or consistently. And this is not just how Pimas are, but how patients are around the globe.

5

Surveillance, Risks, and
''Borderline'' Diabetes

The risk in identifying pregnant women as linchpins of the diabetes epidemic is the greater burden they would bear in the ensuing surveillance. The greater burden of surveillance can only lead to a greater allocation of responsibility for this disease. Surveillance (which already includes standard diabetes screening for all women, more frequent diabetes tests for pregnant Pima women, and possibly self–blood glucose monitoring) is an important component of existing diabetes prevention strategies (fig. 5.1). But this surveillance can be insensitive to the reality of women's lives. Instead, this continuing epidemic is a problem of interpretations. In anthropological terms, this is particularly a conflict between women's semantic illness networks and the terminology of biomedicine.[1] The concepts of "risk" and "borderline" diabetes and the diagnostic process for diabetes during pregnancy mean many things to women undergoing prenatal care. The way women interpret and perceive this typically symptomless form of disease will most strongly determine what health care they seek and when.

Surveillance Risks All Round

Pregnant women are arguably the healthiest people to undergo such frequent and invasive biomedical monitoring as is standard for the prenatal period. This results, in part, from Westerners' growing intolerance for any maternal morbidity, an epidemiological achievement of the last century attributable in large part to biomedical knowledge and technologies. However, the frequent tests create a risk-focused environment in which competing technological, social, and experiential knowledge must coexist (Terry 1989). In this environment, pro-

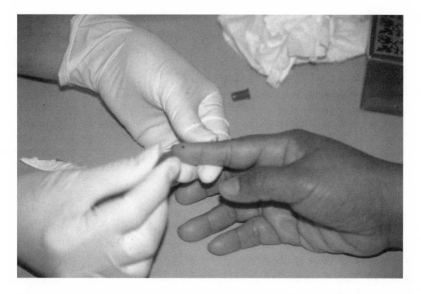

Figure 5.1. Daily glucose monitoring using a drop of blood can be done at home or in the clinic.

fessionals as well as family and friends feel a moral obligation to the fetus as a patient separately identified from the mother (Browner and Sargent 1996). A large body of ethnographic literature explores the limits placed on women's power to make decisions in the prenatal period, especially vis-à-vis that of biomedical practitioners, society, and even the fetus. In this literature, such as the work of Jordan (e.g., 1993, 1997). and the edited volumes on reproduction by Ginsburg and Rapp (1995), and by Davis-Floyd and Sargent (1997), reproduction is viewed as "a microcosm of broader trends" in technologization, medicalization, and even domination, particularly of poor and indigenous women (Davis-Floyd and Sargent 1997:6).[2] Pregnancies at Gila River, especially diabetic pregnancies, have exactly this pan-representational quality. For prenatal diabetes *is* diabetes for and in all Pimas. Diabetes *is* health and illness in nearly all Pimas.

The popularity of biomedically supervised pregnancies and birthing indicates that the majority of women in the United States accept the goals and methods of this approach or are not aware of or cannot exercise other choices.[3] Browner and Press argue that women "want reassurance that they are doing everything possible to reduce 'risk' during pregnancy" (Browner and Press 1997:315). The potential consequences for women who do not fill the role of a good (i.e., compliant, "low risk") patient extend beyond the confines of the clinical encounter. As additional diagnostic tests are made available, women are morally and socially required to submit to them, to avoid the risks they define, and to respond in specific manners to the results. Women who do not subscribe to this standard risk being labeled "bad mothers" or "bad patients" and being otherwise punished through various social mechanisms ranging from shame to legal action against their autonomy and personal freedom.

Screening tests for symptomless or presymptomatic disease—including tests to screen for gestational diabetes, the focus of this research—are the hallmark of epidemiological risk achievements. The ability to identify disease or its precursors before any bodily symptoms are present is a critical advantage in biomedicine and is largely attributable to the population-based research conducted on disease events by epidemiologists. Through epidemiology, characteristics of disease, as well as of diseased populations after and before disease onset, are identified, greatly enhancing our ability to identify, prevent, and provide early treatment for disease. Even a type of postdisease or "remission" state can be identified through screenings when symptoms are under medical control but risk continues. In the case of breast cancer, for example, removal of cysts that may have been precancerous yields not a healthy breast but a cystless one. The patient continues to undergo monitoring for future cyst development and, often, repeat surgeries (see Gifford 1986). It is a thin line between healthy-but-at-risk and diseased. When that boundary is blurred, patients might, for example, see fibrocystic breast disease and breast cancer as different forms of the same disease.

Pima women interpret pregnancy not as disease but as health. For some very good reasons, they interpret diabetes screenings not as definitive assertions but as works in progress. An important interpretive event is when Pima women consider gestational diabetes and "outright" diabetes to be different forms of the same disease. Elimination of GDM (through childbirth) seems to indicate good health. In reality, the infant may be overweight, hypoglycemic, and at higher risk for diabetes; the mother may also be recovering from cesarean section delivery, major surgery with associated risks such as infection, and also at higher risk, herself, for developing outright diabetes.

Testing for GDM has become a standard practice for all pregnant women, not just the Pimas; but it is through these pre- and postdisease windows that risk data expand the purview of biomedical knowledge and authority over pregnant Pima women's experience. Risk data have, therefore, gained a remarkably powerful role in the policing of pregnant bodies. And this is even more so for Pimas, about whom so much diabetes risk information is available. However, risk data do not address the decisions behind prenatal health behaviors. They don't ask "Why?"

Why, for example, might women fail to respond when tests show a risk for GDM? To be tested for GDM at Gila River requires time, persistence, planning, and a strong stomach. The American Diabetes Association (ADA) recommends that all pregnant women receive a risk assessment at the first prenatal visit. For Pima women, this assessment—which checks for marked obesity, personal history of GDM, glycosuria, or a strong family history of diabetes—is considered unnecessary because all Pimas now have some family history of diabetes. The ADA does not recommend further glucose testing for no-risk or low-risk-status women: women who are "less than 25 years old, normal weight before pregnancy, member of an ethnic group with a low prevalence of GDM, no known diabetes in first-degree relatives, no history of abnormal glucose tolerance and no history of poor obstetric outcome" (American Diabetes Association [ADA] 2000). Thus, all Pima women undergo diabetes testing.

The thresholds and measures used in diabetes tests are complex, a challenge for any layperson to understand. I offer a brief outline of the various types of prenatal diabetes screenings for two reasons. First, although Pima women have a high risk for diabetes, they are not different from other diabetes patients who struggle with the generally symptomless nature of diabetes and the lifestyle changes necessary to avoid future health problems. Pima women do not talk about numerical thresholds but about their sense of physical well-being, symptoms, and energy.

Priscilla: If they took care of themselves, you know, they wouldn't get it [diabetes]—and try to maintain a stable weight.

Karen: Just watch what you eat. Yeah, just mainly watch what you eat, that's how I figure.

Diagnostic thresholds that motivate and guide health professionals are of limited value to most Pima women. Second, providers

Table 5.1 Blood sugar thresholds for diagnosis of gestational diabetes mellitus

Timing of blood draw	GCT (mg/dl)[a]	OGTT (mg/dl)[b]
Casual	200 (with complaints)	
Fasting		95
One-hour	126	180
Two-hour	155	155
Three-hour	140	140

Note: GCT = glucose challenge test; OGTT = oral glucose tolerance test
[a]One threshold must be met.
[b]Two thresholds must be met.

are likewise frustrated by the need for multiple glucose readings over time, by the lack of symptoms on which to base a diagnosis, and by the apparent unreceptiveness of patients to behavioral change. Screenings contradict experience; results disobey common sense.

The ADA recommends two methods of diabetes screening for the nonpregnant adult. The first, more simple glucose challenge test (GCT), requires a blood glucose reading of greater than 126 mg/dl after a one-hour fast and duplicated on a subsequent day, or greater than 200 mg/dl from a "casual" blood sample drawn any time and accompanied by complaints of, for example, fatigue, thirst, frequent urination, or blurred vision. These diagnostic thresholds are higher than those for the more complete oral glucose tolerance test (OGTT). The more complex OGTT involves the administration of a glucose "load" (a specified amount of glucose in drink form) and requires four blood checks made at fasting (eight to fourteen hours), one hour, two hours, and three hours. Two or more of the blood sugar concentrations must meet or exceed the diagnostic level for a positive diagnosis (table 5.1).

Screening for diabetes during pregnancy involves a slight modification of these thresholds to include a two-test series. The first test involves a blood sample after a 50-gram glucose load and one-hour (nonfasting) waiting period. At Gila River, all pregnant women are first screened with this test at the first prenatal appointment, ideally between 24 and 26 weeks' gestation, and then again at 32 weeks' gestation. If this test yields a reading of greater than 130 mg/dl, the pregnant woman is referred for the three-hour 100-gram OGTT. If two of the values in the chart below are exceeded (i.e., at fasting, one hour, two hours, and/or three hours), then a diagnosis of gestational diabetes is made. The difference in screenings for pregnant vs. non-pregnant adults is attributable to the changes in glucose metabolism concurrent with pregnancy.

The best-tasting product for these tests, an orange-flavored drink, is used at Gila River and is an important improvement over the nauseating lemon/lime drink of previous years. If the woman cannot hold down the "glucose load," that test must be retaken. The nature of the testing process means that some women may have one test (the 50-gram test) that yields a glucose level above the diagnostic cutoff for gestational diabetes; these women must be willing to undergo the second test in order for a diagnosis to be confirmed. Women may undergo both tests several times during pregnancy and never produce the required two glucose readings above diagnostic threshold, although this is not common. Either way, this is a cumbersome and convoluted diagnostic process for anyone.

The commendable purpose of preventive screening is to identify disease or its precursors. In examining the hegemonic power and social impact of diabetes tests, I am not advocating their removal from standard practice, or even any alteration in the more aggressive preventive measures employed at Gila River. However, the unexamined consequence of this focus on women carries with it some assumptions about what should follow a positive diagnosis.

It is an assumption of biomedicine that patients will then respond accordingly with preventive behaviors outlined by the physician (see Gordon 1988). However, this understanding of screenings is not universal, nor are these responses to test results cross-culturally consistent. One danger in preventive screening is that it can be confused with disease onset. Kavanagh and Broom describe a process whereby women perceive their risk for cancer to have become "activated" through the screening process itself, where no risk existed previous to testing (Kavanagh and Broom 1998:440).[4]

Some Pima women[5] express a similar idea about diabetes becoming activated if one does not "take care" of oneself. Laura,[6] a non-diabetic woman, said, "Part of diabetes is hereditary. And part of it, I think, if they don't take care of themselves, I mean it's like dormant. If I understand it right, to a certain point, you know. And then if you don't take care of yourself it becomes visible or becomes active."

Pregnant Pima women are not atypical in being unsure of how to interpret the results of GDM screenings. It is unclear—since this diabetes is going to "go away" after pregnancy—whether this is something to be concerned about. When I asked Mary whether she had diabetes, she responded in a way common among women.

CS-M: Are you diabetic?
Mary: No. Not that I know of. I don't know—they're still trying to [figure it out]. . . . They said I am, but I don't know. I have to go do some more tests. . . . I didn't know I had diabetes when I was pregnant like with [my first child]. Too, I was—they were saying that I had diabetes too . . . but after they told me I didn't have it.

Mary was diagnosed with GDM during a previous pregnancy. Told after childbirth that her blood sugar level was normal, Mary concluded the original diagnosis had been incorrect. Rather than challenge the permanence of a diagnosis, Mary and many Pima women reasoned that the original decision had been based on some error. Women thereby trust and allow their doctors to "change their diagnosis" rather than view the disease as coming and going.

Because blood sugar levels return to normal after childbirth, a patient is supposed to be reclassified (i.e., retested) after the birth. Yet the ADA definition of GDM reads:

Gestational diabetes mellitus (GDM) is defined as any degree of glucose intolerance with onset or first recognition during pregnancy. The definition applies whether insulin or only diet modification is used for treatment and whether or not the condition persists after pregnancy. It does not exclude the possibility that unrecognized glucose intolerance may have antedated or begun concomitantly with the pregnancy. (ADA 2004)

This definition implies that this GDM is a permanent form of the disease but is simply first noticed or diagnosed during pregnancy. In fact, women are supposed to be retested and reclassified after the pregnancy to confirm the existence of diabetes' permanent form—what Pimas call "outright" diabetes.

The very high rates of diabetes in this community might also influence women to think that diabetes is inevitable. Women say that while diabetes may be in some ways or for some period avoidable, not even the most vigilant and active lifestyle can guarantee avoidance of this disease.

CS-M: Do you think that you will eventually get outright diabetes?

Sarah: When I get older.

CS-M: Do you think that there's any way to avoid it?

Sarah: Um—I wish I could say it would take care [of it]—that (dignity) diet and exercise, [it would] be taken care of, but I don't know.

Another woman summarized what many women said:

Laura: I think it . . . can be avoided for a while, but I think eventually it crops up.

David Kozak has characterized the Pima reaction to decades of increasing prevalence of type 2 diabetes as an attitude of "surrender" to diabetes (Kozak 1997). This reaction is neither apathy nor futility, but a collective response to years of increasing prevalence of diabetes at Gila River despite tremendous financial and clinical investment. Pregnant women's talk about GDM incorporates much of this more general, community-wide reaction to the epidemic; yet they also grappled with the "fickle" blood glucose readings of GDM. Diabetes educators should recognize that pregnant women are, therefore, not always lacking information but are "making sense" (Lang 1989) of a disease that comes, goes, but inevitably comes back to stay.

Countersurveillance Strategies

The sense women make of the diabetes screening process returns us to the question of risk. For many Pima women, no bodily clues to diabetes exist; they have no experience of illness. Risk information fills in where experience leaves off. Risk becomes symptom, is treated as disease, not just as potential. And because symptoms and bodily signs are "malleable," risk lurks in every twitch (Gifford 1986).

So what is an experience of health for Pima women can be redefined as symptomless disease and unhealthy pregnancy. Further, biomedicine conceptualizes pregnancy and diabetes as antagonistic states, the combination of which creates a lifelong period of vulnerability for mother and child. Women are taught that their (diabetic) pregnancy is potentially harmful to their bodies and their baby, and that it will continue to affect them both throughout their lives. Not surprisingly, this unhealthy and risk-laden view of pregnancy is unpopular

and confusing, especially when presented by persons from a "dominant" ethnic category, socioeconomic status, and power position (as is
almost always the case in biomedical institutions on Native American
reservations). Research shows that this confusion is inherent in much
of the "language of risk" for many people, not just Pimas, but is
especially problematic in cross-cultural situations (Gifford 1986).

If prenatal screening is viewed as a vehicle for risk information
and for an ideology of vigilance, it can be seen to pervade Pima wom-
en's experience of pregnancy. Prenatal tests are used by clinicians as
teaching tools, to tie risk with an experience of blood evaluation and
to employ the technological gaze as something women can appreciate
as better than bodily experience. In much of the dominant U.S. medical culture, risk data are considered objective, scientific knowledge to
which patients have the right and through which patients can become
empowered to prevent disease. An individual's sense of vulnerability
to disease is typically informed by professional and lay information as
well as personal experience, and intuition about the likelihood of
developing disease in a given context, time, and circumstance.[7] Comparative risks and optimism also factor into a person's considerations
(van der Pligt 1998). But Pimas have not necessarily been indoctri-
nated into this culture of risk.

Attending prenatal appointments is a crash course in risk and the
appropriate attitude and behaviors in response to it. My discussion
with Florence showed signs of this learning process, as well as moments in which women reject the biomedical approach in favor of
their own ideas. For Florence, "taking care" of herself involved more
than avoiding "risky" behaviors. Florence said, "I think it all depends
on your body, on yourself, on your own thinking. That [you're more
likely to get it if] you're gonna be down and out or all negative."
Attitude had a lot to do with staying well, staving off diabetes, keeping
it "dormant."

Local interpretations of risk information are especially important
in communities with endemic disease and long-standing prevention
programs like Gila River. For example, a low-risk pregnancy among
the Pima is an increasingly rare occurrence. The rise in diabetes prevalence coupled with a falling age of initial diagnosis means that young
Pima women are considered closer in years to a diagnosis of diabetes
than ever before. Monitoring for diabetes during pregnancy is an
advantage women have, one might say, to foreseeing/foretelling their

diabetic future. (One might also call it a disadvantage to females to be responsible for the carriage of diabetes-hastening pregnancy.) However, after their first child, many pregnant women I interviewed were more willing to skip prenatal appointments based on how they were feeling. They expressed greater knowledge of pregnancy and what their bodies were going through, and a greater confidence that they would know if something was wrong. Prenatal visits are seen by these multigravida women as superfluous and inconvenient. Therefore, symptomless gestational diabetes might easily go undiagnosed, as would any symptomless concern. Patricia said she normally attends appointments at the reservation hospital, but hasn't gone much during her current pregnancy because, as she explained, "I think I know what's going on with me."

Related to skipped appointments is women's willingness to alter or abridge prescription directions. Denise's diabetes was out of control during pregnancy, and she was prescribed medication. When she told me that she disagreed with this plan, I asked:

> **CS-M:** Did you complain or were you able to get a second opinion?
> **Denise:** Oh no, I just didn't go cuz I was really upset . . . so I don't go in again.

Denise's is a common belief that pregnancy is "natural" and that medicines are potentially harmful. Neither Denise nor Violet, quoted below, shared these beliefs with her health-care providers.

> **Violet:** Yeah, I felt like they were saying, "Well, you got to take a shot, you gotta take this, you gotta take that." I mean, I didn't really see the need for it. I mean, being pregnant was natural. So I didn't feel like I had to use the medicines.

We can hardly expect women to announce their noncompliance. But it is appropriate to ask whether women would ask questions or discuss a treatment plan that troubled them. Of the 63 participants interviewed, 39 (roughly two-thirds) said they would say or do nothing if they disagreed with their doctor; 4 would switch doctors without speaking up; and 18 said they would initiate a conversation or ask further questions in response to feelings of disagreement (two participants offered no response to this question). This "lack of assertiveness with physicians" has also been documented among Mexican Americans (Larme and Pugh 2001). The strategies of secretive noncompliance and skipping appointments are important factors in the failure of diabetes prevention.

Yet these purposeful ("noncompliant") actions do not explain all Pima behaviors. To be fair, not all poor communication is intentional, and I will discuss communication further in chapter 7. But if women's strategy for coping with disagreement is to keep concerns hidden or to skip appointments, then this behavior may be more common around GDM screenings for which the diagnosis appears unreliable. These quotes also reveal potential problems for women taking (or directed to take) insulin or other medications to control blood glucose during pregnancy.

The Nondiagnosis of "Borderline"

The apparently "fickle" nature of GDM combines with the sometimes limited two-way communication about GDM to generate semantic disagreement, if not "outright" disagreement, about the nature of diabetes. In response to the question "What do you think it means to be 'at risk'?," the most common response involved the term "borderline."

> **Maureen:** I don't know because . . . you know people that had been told they were a borderline candidate—here, you know, because . . . I've talked to different people, and they have different reactions. So what does that mean, borderline? Either you are or you aren't!

> **CS-M:** What do you think it means to be at risk for diabetes?
> **Priscilla:** That they were borderline.

> **CS-M:** What do you think it means to be at risk for diabetes?
> **Denise:** Just, is that like another term for borderline?

Women's words below reveal how the term "borderline" is used to negotiate and understand the various forms of diabetes—particularly gestational diabetes. Although she says she was diagnosed with diabetes four years ago, the fact that the term "borderline" was used leaves her uncertain as to whether she has it or not.

> [I think I'll get it] when I get older [though I don't have it now]. . . . About four years ago I was diagnosed with diabetes. I have borderline diabetes. [But] someone told me, you either are or you're not, there is no borderline.

Some Pimas who are tested over a period of time show a progressive rise in their glucose readings, furthering the cultural meaningfulness of the linear progress and the idea of a "borderline diabetic." Women expect their numbers to become progressively higher in a fairly consistent manner over the course of their lives. The belief expressed in Sarah's quote above, that if you control what you eat, you can avoid diabetes, cannot be guaranteed. If women believed this, or were told this by a caregiver, and subsequently developed diabetes when their diet was good, they may come to doubt prevention messages altogether.

Although these terms are used to help explain diabetes, they often mislead patients. Since diabetes is diagnosed with the use of a numerical scale indicating a blood glucose level—if your reading is above x number, you have diabetes; if not, you don't—then numbers close to the diagnostic cutoff are often described as "borderline." Women who receive diagnoses of gestational diabetes are more likely to use the term "borderline." Further, these blood glucose numbers fluctuate all the time. So a reading one day might be well within diabetic range, while the next day may be normal. The term "borderline" also incorporates the transitive nature of these numbers, allowing one or a few "over the cutoff" numbers before a diagnosis is firmly established. Doctors and other providers at Gila River grimace at the use of this lay interpretation, because they recognize the complacency and hedging that it produces.

As the outcome study at Gila River and other data show, education is correlated with controlled blood sugar, an important factor in the future health of mother and baby. Increased testing of pregnant Pima women is a very reasonable prevention strategy, given the tribe's high prevalence of diabetes. But women's reactions to and interpretations of the GDM test may actually contribute to no-shows and noncompliance. Specific contribution factors include: the difficulty of completing and possible contradictions between the necessary multiple tests; the apparent fickleness of a diagnosis that is often changed after birth; and a variety of cultural and economic barriers to health care that pregnant women share with all Pimas. Once involved in health care, women's communication with and relationships to providers will also impact their attendance and adherence to treatment. To explore communication, we must consider the provider's perspective as well.

Part III

6

Two Hands Shaking

My conversations with Pima women and health care providers alike, on impersonal subjects—the etiology of diabetes, the meaning of medical tests, and so on—were replete with remarks and stories about people. Pimas talked quite a bit about providers, some they liked and others they disliked. Providers likewise talked about their patients, sometimes in familiar terms and other times as an anonymous "population" or "patient group." Put side by side, the assortment of Pima and provider stories reveals some of the commonplace problems in the prevention and treatment of chronic disease in our health care system.

On the One Hand

Hard at their work, the health care providers at Gila River might be surprised to hear some of women's complaints. They described their Pima patients to me in placid terms: very pleasant, friendly, laid-back. Almost all of them are enthusiastic about their jobs and their daily interactions with patients. Several even attend community events outside of work and feel intense devotion to the people of Gila River. Of course, it is also possible to find providers like those about whom women complained. Describing Pimas as "apathetic," "challenging," and even "passive-aggressive," there are those who would put the blame for out-of-control diabetes squarely and simply on Pimas. Nevertheless, the majority know and acknowledge the effects of economics and history on Pima subsistence and lifestyle. One summarized it this way in a brief written questionnaire I collected:

> [Pimas are] caught between traditional values and encroaching urban-ism. Many social strengths: they know their history—can "count" on each other. Also many social problems related to clash

and cultural valueless/situations: predominantly poverty, DM (diabetes mellitus), alcoholism, and depression.

Of the 16 professionals who completed written questionnaires— the method they preferred over interviews because of time constraints —fourteen agreed that cultural knowledge was essential to their ability to provide good health care. One notable exception was the woman who, despite years of service to the community, a position of authority, and presumed learning on the subject, said to me, "Culture? There's no culture here. That's just something they say to get what they want from whites." No one else spoke (or wrote) with such contempt for or ignorance of Pima culture, but there were several who said Pima culture was "dead" or "thrown away." For these providers, culture is not seen as a living and changing thing—as if to say that if Pimas are no longer farming and living in *olás ké* (round houses made of brush and timbers), they aren't really Pimas. The debates about authenticity and traditionalism in Native Americans are quite old but surged in the 1970s in response to indigenous activism and increasing tribal enrollments. Since then, such challenges to Indian authenticity have primarily been viewed as an instrument of acculturation and exclusion (see especially Nagel 1996; Goldberg-Ambrose 1994). A more correct understanding of Pima culture recognizes that Pimas have changed and adapted since time immemorial, as have all extant cultures.

What providers know about Pima culture comes largely from what they learn from patients, plus the brief orientation given to them as new employees of the hospital. Following are several responses to a question on what providers know of the Pima culture:

- Non-Indian, 13 years in the community: Read a great deal, attend meetings so know more, attend cultural events outside of work.
- Non-Indian, 1 ½ years in the community: Not enough. The [orientation] film we saw was so old it was ridiculous. The Casa Grande Ruins [a nearby Hohokam archaeological site and park] has a much more up-to-date visual. I need to spend more time learning—just don't know when.
- Non-Indian, 1 year in the community: Very little.
- Non-Indian, 14 years in the community: Long history, some words and expressions, tried many Pima foods, attend cultural events including church and funeral traditions, extensive.

In short, although they may not get it in a new employee orientation, a provider can learn quite a bit about Pima culture after spending some time on the reservation.

To contrast with Pimas' explanations of the barriers they perceive to obtaining good care—things such as treatment and respect by providers, transportation, and child care—I also asked providers what they thought was "the single most important barrier to better health in this community." About two-thirds of providers thought the diabetes problem was in individual patients whose "obesity" (n = 2), "apathy" (n = 1), "lack of motivation" (n = 2), or inadequate education (n = 4) explained their "failure to fully realize the importance of diet and exercise to maintain health." (Not all of the two-thirds were quoted in that sentence.) Of the remaining seven clinicians, four said the problem was with the medical facilities or with "doctors who don't spend time listening or just attribute client symptoms to age or state of their diabetes without looking into the situation further." The other three cited economic issues (including transportation limitations) as the greatest barrier to Pimas seeking and following treatment.

A survey questionnaire is an undesirable tool to many ethnographers because of its tendency to oversimplify people's responses to complex questions. The data from my survey of hospital providers risk the same problem. But my discussions with these providers indicate that they are clearly aware of the larger context of disease. Providers aren't typically in a position to change the political and economic factors keeping Pimas in poverty, unemployment, and ill health. What they can and do try to impact, however, is how well they communicate with their patients and whether, once received at a health care appointment, patients are convinced of the meaningfulness and benefits of continuing with care. With few exceptions, providers at Gila River try to make their patients feel informed, respected, and involved in an effective and practical treatment plan. For this communication, providers must be informed and sensitive about cultural modes of communication.

How to be heard: this is the challenge of diabetes clinicians here, if not everywhere. How to get a convincing and motivating message across, and to know when you've done it. Asked, "How do you know your patients listen to and follow your instructions?," Gila River providers described patients who engage them in conversation about treatment, "ask questions" or for clarification, "verbalize the instructions back to me," and are "attentive." These are all recognizable cues within the dominant medical culture. But these perceptions are not appropriate for some Pimas who, as I will discuss in the next chapter, demonstrate respect or deference to authority through silence and avoidance of eye contact. Providers experiencing these traits in their patients are more likely to interpret them as apathy or lack of motivation. One of these providers, answering how he knew his patients listened and followed instructions, said simply, "I don't think they do."

These findings do not differ greatly from other studies of diabetes providers. Larme and Pugh outline nine qualitative themes for why diabetes is so much harder to treat than other diseases (1998). They include: the limitations of medications for controlling the disease; the labor intensity required to control the constant fluctuations of blood glucose levels; the fact that lifestyle changes are outside of provider control; the difficulty in treating symptomless disease with medications that can produce negative symptoms; the professional controversies over how to manage diabetes effectively; the inexorable decline of the patient; and the extra time and expense for limited reimbursement (1998; see also Hunt, Arar, and Larme 1998; Larme and Pugh 2001).

I also asked providers to address the semantic problems associated with the term "borderline" and the concepts of "risk." Providers are clear and unanimous about the term "borderline" and had this to say about its use in clinical practice:

> No! No! No!

> No—don't use it. It's like being "a little pregnant." I prefer to use the term "early diabetes."

> Patients seem to use this term and have their own understanding of what that means.

> Borderline is not a recognizable medical diagnosis.

> No. You either are diabetic or not diabetic.

They also were much more comfortable with the concept of risk. They explained:

> It depends on who I'm talking to. Some clients seem really interested, others have the attitude that it won't happen to them.

> We discuss risks for diabetes. Almost all patients are very concerned about their risk of diabetes and they want info. about how to avoid becoming diabetic.

Some patients state it is the first time they've heard this [risk information] and seem to be concerned and want to make changes —Others say, "I know, I know . . . I hear this all the time" and don't seem to want to change.

Pimas equated a state of being "at risk" for diabetes with being "borderline" or on the verge of an "outright" diabetes diagnosis. For providers, being "at risk" applies to *all* Pimas, including ones far from a diagnosis.

But that is the problem. If Pimas feel a discussion of risk is actually a discussion of disease they essentially already have, then their expectations for how that discussion is handled will differ significantly from their provider's expectations.

A hypothetical death sentence is a vastly different conversation than a real death sentence.

On the Other Hand

The high utilization of biomedical services on the Gila River Indian Reservation is testimony to its efficacy. But, as with the Dakota, biomedicine is considered part of what Pimas consider "the 'outside' white or majority society" (Lang 1989:320). Thus, Pima ideas about "good" health care are not always about the treatment services provided. While the biomedical model is widely accepted on the Gila River Indian Reservation, evidenced by full schedules at the hospital and clinic,[1] these patterns hide a variety of local differences in the way biomedicine is used, interpreted, and evaluated.

The common strategies of Pima women dealing with problematic issues of health care included switching providers and refraining from going in for care at all. Refusing care is particularly common when women have already "tried" two care providers, since the number of staff is limited and women begin to believe, after two attempts, that no better care is available. Olivia, who did go in for prenatal care fairly regularly during the current pregnancy, believes she did what most Pimas would do when she switched doctors without making her complaints known.

CS-M: What do you do if you disagree with your doctor?
Olivia: I don't know.
CS-M: Have you ever?
Olivia: No, not really. There's this one doctor I had that I didn't really care for . . .

CS-M: Did you have to see her every time, or were you able to get a different one?
Olivia: Yeah, I got a different one.
CS-M: Did you ask for a different one?
Olivia: Yeah.
CS-M: So then, did you ever say anything to her directly or not?
Olivia: No.
CS-M: And do you think that you handled that situation pretty much how most people would, or do you think you handled it differently?
Olivia: Probably how most people would, get a different doctor.
CS-M: And not say anything?
Olivia: Yeah.

While this approach is certainly not unique to Pima women, it demonstrates how caregivers may not know when they've alienated a patient.

We cannot forget, also, that pregnancy is, for many women, a very fatiguing experience. Not only is the body's energy being directed to produce and nurture the fetus, but there is added weight to carry, a higher body temperature, and sometimes nausea, to name a few issues. Reluctance of pregnant women to ask questions is, thus, not always a relationship problem but a normal result of fatigue that comes with pregnancy, as in Ethel's case:

Sometimes [I've left the doctor's office confused], and then when I try to go back, they're either with a different patient or I'll have to wait, and I can't wait. I mean, I don't got the patience for it, especially when I'm pregnant. . . . I do that a lot. Like, they'll be saying things, and I'll come home and tell my husband what they said. And he'll say, "What is that?" or "What do they mean"? And I'll say, "I don't know. I didn't ask them." . . . I think I just forget [to ask]. . . . And I don't realize what they say, or sometimes I'm just not listening. I'm upset or I'm tired, and I just don't want to sit there and wait to hear their answers, so I just don't say nothing. I just go home and get mad at my own husband when he tries to ask me [what they meant].

Patients who "ask questions," "appear attentive and interact," or "further go into detail about the problem" are considered to be listening and engaged. However, many Pimas are more quiet and unquestioning as a sign of respect and deference, especially when the setting is very formal or rushed, as is often the case. Pimas' silence may initially be unrelated to a relationship or communication problem— but may grow into one if providers and patients cannot develop a more open and trusting relationship. These findings echo other reports that Native Americans avoid confrontation, especially with authority figures (see Lang 1989; see Philips 1983). Others, like Ethel, don't know what to ask, or forget to ask during the rushed appointments. Further, many Pimas will avoid direct or prolonged eye contact, especially with strangers or persons in authority. This practice, which is intended to show respect, is distinctly contrary to caregivers' expectations. Among Warm Springs Indian children, a teacher's fixed gaze conveys "hostility of much greater intensity than among Anglos" (Philips 1983:107). Also, the desire not to appear foolish or to show deference to authority is characteristic of many Native American cultures (Lazarus 1997). However, these traits may be met with irritation, hostility, or apathy from non-Indian providers who do not recognize these cultural differences between themselves and their patients.

Trying to Shake Hands

As Szurek found among birthing women in Italy, "when a woman enters a hospital for childbirth, it is assumed that she is already socialized to obey the rules" (Szurek 1997:296). Women in labor are admitted, disrobed, laid on a flat bed, and expected to refrain from pushing until a doctor arrives to give approval. Beliefs that don't conform to the implied rules are seen as intentionally disruptive, noncompliant, etc. when, in fact, they may not be intentional. The same is true in U.S. hospitals, even in the heart of "Indian Country," and the receptionist regularly greets patients in their native language. Biomedical rules of behavior, including where to be, what information to report, and when to speak or not speak, are often presumed when, in truth, significant differences exist between Pima and non-Indian expectations for clinical interactions.

Providers, especially those new to the reservation, have ample evidence of missed appointments upon which to base assumptions about Pima noncompliance. But poor compliance and resistance to biomedicine's efforts to improve the health in a community are not limited to Gila River. These problems are ubiquitous, occurring in everything from vaccination campaigns in the remotest of development encounters to managed care in a fully industrialized society. Noncompliance also varies over time as women interact with biomedical providers differently through their life span, depending upon such things as the type and severity of symptoms, age, experiences with health care in the past, and access.

Studies into the way indigenous communities accept and utilize biomedical health care reveal an intricate web of values that bind biomedicine with dominant U.S. culture (see Daviss 1997). Social change itself has important negative consequences for these communities, particularly if it is an indigenous one (Joe and Young 1994; Kunitz 1983; Lang 1989). Values about individualized patient care, the proper sick role, and access to care uphold biomedical assumptions and practices.[2] So while biomedicine "helps people adapt to a changing world by providing scientific legitimacy for new ways of acting, by defining new problems, and by redefining old ones" (Kunitz 1983:186), it can also be destructive to indigenous and traditional forms of knowledge, not of necessity, but due to biomedicine's intolerance for other ways of knowing (Davis-Floyd and Sargent 1997; Daviss 1997; O'Neil and Kaufert 1995; Pearce 1993). Biomedicine might even act as an acculturative agent, because it is often one of the first elements of Western culture to be delivered to remote and Third World communities.

Diabetes care is already individualized by providers who are deeply invested in the success of their patients; the services of numerous personnel are coordinated through case management work done through the Diabetes Education Center and by the providers themselves when necessary. Transportation to appointments is made available, inexpensive food substitutions are offered in diabetes cooking classes, and Pimas have access to both individual and group settings for diabetes care, monitoring, and treatment. But returning to the potential interactional impasses between Pimas and their providers, we are reminded of the importance of culture, upbringing, and the familiarity that time brings between two speakers. Asking questions of an authority figure is part of the linguistic "competence" gained through enculturation (Hymes 1967; Goodenough 1976). Averting one's eyes from a speaker's confrontational gaze has been discussed by Philips (1983). The subtleties of linguistic competence are not learned quickly and are especially difficult to pinpoint when speakers share a common language. They are gained through a "developmental sequence" and a particular context, which is sometimes incorrectly assumed to be universal for all members of a society (Philips 1983:4).

The physician has formal authority over the sequence of the clinical encounter. The flow and structure of the health care encounter become symbolic of the authority of the physician. The physician's authority over the interview process is vested in her or his title or licensure. Technically, these privileges apply to physicians who are licensed by the state and practice within that license. So, as Gramsci identified the "school" (including the medical school) as a state institution for perpetuating the ideology of the elites (1971:258), so too on a face-to-face level of interaction is the medical interview a format for instilling this ideology into patients. Thus, Pima women are taught the role of a good patient through the regular interactions of doctor visits. Women learn through each encounter with biomedical providers what is expected of them and what the rules of the clinical interaction are. These rules include addressing only biomedically significant symptoms, minimizing elaboration into social, economic, and other nonmedical concerns, and not asking too many questions. Too much intrusion or abridgment of this process would be considered chaotic and unacceptable.

Dismantling this hierarchy of authority are those practices that balance the role of provider and patient in clinical care, particularly in the development of the treatment plan. Diabetes care in the United States has always been based on the standards of care set by the ADA, which, while stating that "the management plan should be formulated in collaboration with the patient," are focused exclusively on biological end points (Wolpert and Anderson 2001). That is, treatment plans are written with biological measures—for example, reductions in A1c or weight—as the treatment goal. But the most effective physicians, at Gila River and elsewhere, recognize that patients are influenced by the environment they live in: family interactions, the broader social and cultural community, and socioeconomic and health care system factors (Wolpert and Anderson 2001).

Physician attitudes and practices have changed somewhat in recent decades, from those of a more impersonal expert adviser to those of a motivational counselor and expert resource. Doctors are now recognizing that patients may feel that their personal autonomy (and not just their blood sugar levels) are being attacked by relentless, decontextualized exhortations of their physician. In the extreme case, "the initial dilemma of whether or not to snack can be suppressed by the more general disagreements over the support provider's right or need to make such suggestions" (Coyne et al. 1988; Wolpert and Anderson 2001).

> With most doctors, the agenda of patients' visits is usually focused on the technicalities of diabetes management; in practice this usually means advising the patient what they need to do to improve glucose control. However, as pointed out by the originators of motivational interviewing, giving advice is rarely effective in changing selfcare practices. (Miller and Rollnick 1991; Wolpert and Anderson 2001)

Thus, overemphasis on numeric goals, while ignoring the current economic, social, and cultural barriers faced by the patient, can lead to interactive habits between providers and patients that are counterproductive to treatment goals (Wolpert and Anderson 2001).

Relinquishing the ideal as the goal of treatment might seem to physicians like an abomination under the Hippocratic oath. But realistic and attainable goals "foster a sense of success, competence, and engagement that can drive greater improvements" (Wolpert and Anderson 2001:995), thus making care more effective, making patients more successful, and making the work of physicians far more beneficial. In this light, exercises like self-monitoring of blood glucose—a mainstay of current ADA guided treatment plans—might even be relinquished altogether for patients shown not to benefit from it in terms of glucose control (i.e., those not on insulin therapy who can immediately respond with an insulin dose to suboptimal readings) (Franciosi et al. 2001). For the elderly, provider attention to their patients' ability to pay for both medications and monitoring materials, or to diabetes symptoms easily regarded as normal aging, can improve the ultimate outcome (Skelly 2002). As told to me by one registered-nurse friend who worked on a large, randomized clinical trial to prevent diabetes, "whatever it takes." In that successful and popular trial, participants who made lifestyle changes through diet and exercise reduced their risk of getting type 2 diabetes by 58 percent (Knowler et al. 2002).

Anthropological research has indicated other ways in which physicians can "control" therapeutic communication. In one study of therapeutic discussions with elderly patients, physicians were shown to actively rather than passively interrupt, introduce stories, become precise, and "bridge" for the purpose of "maintain[ing] control of the interview" (Katz 1984:100–103). A physician friend of mine tells me it takes less than seven seconds on average for doctors to interrupt their patients.

Another area of effort for which experts should be credited is "translational research," in which research energies are invested to make scientific advances more useful in places like Gila River. Convinced that blood glucose control can reduce health problems, and that healthy diet and exercise can delay or prevent the development of diabetes, these experts work to "translate" the achievements of clinical research into "real-world practice" (Garfield et al. 2003). Among their priorities are:

- moving from an acute-care paradigm to a multifaceted chronic-care model that is population-based, proactive, and patient-centered
- community-based participatory translational efforts involving partnerships among researchers, community members, and governmental/private agencies
- public health and policy efforts (Garfield et al. 2003)

Now, while this is no dismantling of the biomedical power structure, it does demonstrate a shift away from hospital-based, acute care toward efforts that are more community based.

And Pimas have their own brand of control. "Stubbornness" and being "hardheaded" are often associated with elders and the more "traditional" types who refuse not only biomedical care but some other reservation "imports," like the English language, bank accounts, and BIA housing. However, it also became apparent that the word *stubborn* was being used euphemistically for anyone who was intolerant of poor treatment, long waits, or the confusing nature of some biomedical services.

> **CCS-M:** Why do you think some Pimas don't like going to the doctor?
> **Sara:** Stubborn, that's how they were brought up. That's how my grandma was. . . . She didn't like going to the doctor till she was real real sick, and then she figured it'll go away or "I can cure it," you know.

Being "stubborn" means you have decided to reject medical care; the term was never applied to people who "stubbornly" attended appointments or followed carefully the prescriptions of doctors.

Women's use of this term implies if not a moral message about refusing health care, then at least an effort to impress upon me their
disapproval. The characterization of being "stubborn" makes patients' intolerance of unreasonable treatment into a personality trait.
It draws attention away from other reasons for avoiding care.

Indicators that communication is stifled are themselves ambig-
uous. For example, the expression "some way" is sometimes used by
Pimas in response to the routine question, "How are you feeling?"
This term can mean "fine, not too bad"; it can refer to a specific,
uncomfortable symptom that a person can and would describe further if asked to do so; it can reflect patient uncertainty about some or
all aspects of a given discomfort; or it can be used intentionally for
ambiguity, when the patient is reluctant to describe the problem in
that setting, time, or relationship. Non-Indian caregivers have confused the meaning of this response or have considered it a non-
response that indicates a generalized distrust of health care. Instead,
use of the phrase "some way" may simply mean the patient doesn't
know how to describe it differently, may need help or encouragement
to speak freely, or may need an alternative provider with whom they
feel more comfortable.[3] Caregivers must be able to communicate well
enough to get patients to communicate in turn. Two-way, nonconfrontational communication facilitates learning.

Communication patterns in Pima homes might shed some light
on the patient/healer interaction. Diabetes is rarely discussed at
home, especially among family members who do not have the disease.
There is little "prevention talk" between family members. In fact,
Laura was the first of many women to explain to me the taboo against
speaking about diabetes in some families:

> The amputations, and diabetes, and the dialysis—yeah, dialysis.
> Some would rather die than go on it. . . . Yeah, and then they just
> want to die, and they give up. They just give up, but a lot of
> people, that's why we don't talk about diabetes. It wasn't talked
> about much when I was growing up. It was, like, taboo. It's the
> disease that had a really bad stigmatism [sic] to its name.

Where diabetes is not taboo is in the schools, at memorials, gatherings of elders (e.g., at community centers), and other events where
health is a common topic of concern. Rarely or never did women
discuss nutrition or diet at home with family members. Occasionally,

parents may tell children not to eat too many sweets or chips, but, in general, there is not a "family approach" to nutrition or exercise. Education on these topics is left for the schools or hospitals.

> **Vina:** We don't talk about nutrition, but we talk. . . . It would be a little weird. We don't usually hear that.

> **CS-M:** How do Pima kids learn about health and what's good for them?
> **Olivia:** School.
> **CS-M:** So, what do they learn in school that you know of?
> **Olivia:** What's good for them, like vegetables.
> **CS-M:** OK, so nutrition. How about any other topics?
> **Olivia:** Brushing their teeth. They always come home . . . brushing their teeth.
> **CS-M:** Do you think that nutrition is talked about at home?
> **Olivia:** No. . . . [It would] probably be weird for them, because they never hear us talk about things like that.

Is it possible that this cultural feature—how children are taught about nutrition—is in transition, since some women say they were taught about nutrition as a child, but have since developed unhealthy eating habits? Olivia went on to explain, "I don't know, yeah, my mom did [teach me about nutrition], I guess. I used to eat real good when I was small, but I'm not sure what happened." And when education does occur in the home, it is more often by modeling than by explicit discussion. Sometimes, it is the child educating the parent!

> **CS-M:** How do Pima kids learn about health and what's good for them?
> **Betty:** Mainly from school and TV, I guess.
> **CS-M:** What kinds of things do they learn in school, for example?
> **Betty:** Brush your teeth, taking showers, and stuff like that.
> **CS-M:** Anything else? Do they learn anything from home?
> **Betty:** Yeah, well, it depends on the parents. I guess it depends on them—how they are—if they're drinkers or stuff like that. . . .

> **CS-M:** How do Pima kids learn about health and what's good for them?
> **Vina:** Sometimes they're taught through school. My niece, she's taught . . . they give her, like, papers or, like, food charts, and they tell them what they should eat. So she's learning.

CS-M: Where do Pima kids learn about health?
Mariline: I think their classes . . . and then that little school like with the Quest [health and nutrition] program and then . . . Head Start . . . they see like a lot of demonstrations.
CS-M: Do people talk about it at home?
Mariline: I don't know sometimes, like, when they see, you know, have classes at school, my kids bring it home. That's where I get mostly all my information from, is my kids . . . all my kids always . . . bring me lot of information.

Information shared by children filters up through the age groups and is used by adults and elders to interpret the signs and symptoms of experience. This information is then added to other diagnostic information—for example, glucose test numbers—on an ongoing basis to produce an individual's behaviors.

Intergenerational communication is thus an important mechanism through which information is transmitted. If adult diabetes education classes do not reach a substantial portion of Pimas, but children and parents are discussing what kids learn in school, then perhaps an intergenerational approach to communication should be exploited for diabetes prevention. People may feel more comfortable asking questions and expressing doubts and concerns among family than to professionals. Home-based or family-focused approaches would resolve the problems created by lack of transportation, long waits in the hospital waiting room, and confidentiality issues. Indeed, this was suggested by Pima women themselves:

Zinah: I think they should have more home visits just in case, like you're sick, you don't want to go to the doctor for it. Like, come around or call more, like every day or every other day check on you. . . . That's why I don't like when I go . . . cuz I don't have an appointment. Seems like, seems like three to four hours before you get to the doctor, and sometimes you're really sick.

CS-M: Do you feel that the tribe is doing enough about diabetes?
Eileen: I think they should do a little bit more. Get more people out here to do what you're doing.
CS-M: Come out to the houses?
Eileen: Yeah, get more involved.
CS-M: That's kind of what field nurses do too. You know, they're nurses that come to the houses.
Eileen: Yeah, I would like that.

The most positive women were those who had identified a provider with whom they felt comfortable to speak openly and to ask questions of, and who would provide them the information and the effective medications they needed. In particular, they confirmed the importance of longevity, discussed in regard to DEC enrollment problems, as important to feelings about care and willingness to attend appointments.

Dorothy: There's turnovers. . . . I try to always get Dr. A, but sometimes she's not always available. . . . I seen her last time, yeah. That's why we don't really want to see your own doctor then try to see another doctor when she's not there anymore. Dr. A, she's been there for a long time.

Tricia: Yeah. But like now, I was so used to, I had a regular doctor and she was a lady doctor, and she was real good with me. But now with this pregnancy when I tried to go back and see her, she's really booked up. And if I was to get a prenatal appointment, my first prenatal probably won't be until the end of this month, or the beginning of March. . . . Yeah, I think the ones who have been here, who maybe worked here for ten years or something, they obviously worked with the Pimas . . . they talk.

Martha: Yeah, there are certain people that are real civil, if you know who to go to, they'll treat you right.

Turnover of hospital staff makes the development of trust harder. And since Indians living on reservations are more stationary than non-Indian providers, some patients may not understand or appreciate the greater mobility of non-Indian providers. While residencies and short-term placements are a well-established tradition in the profession of biomedical care, this type of movement might be viewed by Indians living on the reservation as abnormal, a rejection of the community in favor of another place, a rejection of community members in favor of a healthier population, or a difficulty with the hospital itself. One provider said this:

They seem to listen, but all the discussion by med providers will never be effective until the community awareness and knowledge of the disease is communicated *between* community members! [emphasis mine]

From insights about linguistic and cultural competence, we must finally recognize the context of power in which patients and providers operate. Away from the hospital and clinic, Pima women are driven more by symptoms and logistical constraints than by biomedical priorities. Gestational diabetes is rarely discussed outside of health care settings. Experiential knowledge competes most heavily with biomedicine for women's time and energy—a form of knowledge that relies heavily on symptomatology that is not usually present in this form of diabetes. Providers' time is stretched thin to manage a large volume of both scheduled and walk-in patients. They feel unempowered, if not simply unable, to make community-wide changes because of their own caseload, the need for more case management to help patients manage their social and economic barriers, and hierarchical and political barriers that keep them from implementing what they feel are innovative and effective ideas.

All of these problems blend into the even larger context of Indian health care and the history of political and economic inequality that all Native Americans face. Treatment must be practical within the community setting. Health interventions cannot be seen as overly intense, much less disciplinary or critical. As Florence's comment reinforces, to get "all down and negative" is a sure path to disease. According to Pimas, the goal is, simply, to "take care of yourself" even if diabetes does "eventually crop up." Provider advice and treatment has to mesh with this attitude.

Providers feel most successful when patients share personal experiences, concerns, and "intimate things," when they smile, and "when they come back." Some providers claim fondly the patients who call and ask specifically for them, or who refer their family and friends to see them. There is a good deal of hugging, handshaking, laughter, and joking between patients and their favored providers, despite the tremendous burden of chronic disease on these relationships. For these successful providers, no-shows are probably lower. For others:

- There is a large no-show rate.
- Most don't seek care in a timely manner—they tend to be seen only after.
- Our DNKAs [number of patients who "Did Not Keep Appointment"] are pretty high.

This leaves at least one provider feeling like "this population is overly dependent on the health care system. They seek care for minor afflictions while avoiding care for major chronic conditions."

Almost unanimously, providers know "it takes time to get comfortable and for [Pimas] to accept you." A few are willing to invest that time and have met with great success, both medically in reduced morbidity and interpersonally. These providers are the ones most eager to see a net reduction in diabetes and, not surprisingly, are the ones most eager to improve their (already good) communication with Pima patients.

Nevertheless, providers and patients have together arrived at some "best practices," strategies that worked to put Pimas at ease and to help providers and patients develop a practical and successful treatment plan.

- Treat every patient the same with attention, respect, and dignity. Listen. Don't pass the buck. Try to help each person or if you pass them on, be sure they were taken care of. (Registered Nurse)
- Attempt to praise and encourage even small positive changes in behavior regarding their health. (Doctor)
- Being flexible is probably the most helpful approach. (Doctor)
- [The best practice is] Working with a family in a community setting on a one-to-one basis (Well-Child clinic)

And most important:

- To relax, remain low key. (Family Nurse Practitioner)

7

Treatment(s)

The first goal of treatment of type 2 diabetes is glycemic control—getting blood sugar levels under control through a combination of monitoring, diet, exercise, and possibly medication. Medications may include insulin, oral hypoglycemics (which stimulate the pancreas to release insulin), insulin sensitizers (which increase the sensitivity of tissues to insulin), starch blockers (which slow the digestion of starches), and metformin (Glucophage®, which decreases the production of glucose by the liver and increases the utilization of glucose from tissues).

Treatment also involves the management and prevention of complications. Blood pressure and blood lipids are monitored and managed. Patient behaviors such as smoking, not to mention eating and exercise, come under greater scrutiny and direction. Careful attention is given to the eyes and feet. And preconceptual counseling is advised by the ADA for all patients with diabetes. Special guidelines exist for elderly, young, and adolescent patients.

How to Treat People with Diabetes

The clinical folks at Gila River are fiercely devoted to their patients and their work. They struggle every day to be effective, caring, accessible, and approachable to their patients, bridging a cultural gap that is widened not only by the cultural and personal differences separating them from their patients, but also by the tragic unfairness and nastiness of diabetes, about which no one likes to talk, especially in the first person.

Although I used the Diabetes Education Center as my home base during fieldwork, I spent much of my hospital time at the prenatal clinic. It was there that I met many of my pregnant informants and spoke most with providers about the intricacies and complications of prenatal diabetes. The prenatal clinic staff are some of the most important providers on the reservation, if we are to take seriously the implications of gestational diabetes for the mother and fetus. And they do. Set off from the main hospital building in their own, new building, the "purple team" is a small and intimate band. Not always in agreement about behind-the-scenes logistics and bureaucracy, these nurses, doctors, and administrative staff were cohesive, intelligent, and responsive in providing care. The nurses seemed to know every single pregnant woman on sight and by name, even knew some details about her family and life at home. Each one had the various test thresholds, symptoms, and diagnostic cues memorized for immediate assessment of any crisis, particularly those related to diabetes in pregnancy. They seemed to me expert in referrals, navigating within and across hospitals to place their patients at the hospital of choice for delivery or for other needed prenatal services. Reports at both ends of the diabetes referral chain—here in prenatal and over at the DEC—were that few if any pregnant women were ever missed. All were tested and all warranting referrals were given one. In some cases, I watched nurses escort women over to the DEC themselves—chatting and laughing on the way.

Joan was a particular inspiration. Not a Pima, Joan was one of those tribal employees that made her job her second home. It was hard to imagine her life outside of work, though of course she had one. She had her own, grown children and a husband about whom she talked regularly. But she was simply immersed in her work and in her patients. Names and details about patients' other children and their whereabouts came flowing out of Joan's mouth with such speed and familiarity, I often wondered how often she got out of the hospital. But like many nontribal employees at the hospital, those expeditions were rare for Joan: the occasional memorial service or holiday parade. Even so, Joan retained what people told her, gave her patients an immediate sense of belonging in the clinic, and along with a few others like her, went a long way to bridging the cultural differences between patients and their clinics.

I had less contact with most doctors. From patients, I learned that one of the most popular doctors was also a basketball player who shared stories of the sport with her patients. This doctor's popularity was attributable to her manner, her familiarity on and off the reservation, and the time she took to involve herself in the lives of her patients—not simply their medical records. She was the same doctor who would later conceive of and start a group format for appointments to which many Pimas have enthusiastically responded. She devotes an entire morning to an assembled group of patients, answering both individual and general questions. Patients benefit from the more social atmosphere, without relinquishing the one-to-one time that the doctor also offers as part of the schedule.

Another young doctor, Indian but not Pima and wearing a long braid down his back, invited me to observe his acupuncture clinic, where he treated a variety of disorders. The day I observed, there was an obese woman with poor circulation in her knees and calves, a man with difficulty breathing and pain in his chest, and a woman with arthritis who was recovering from surgery on one of her hands. For these ailments, the doctor administered several carefully placed acupuncture needles, some of them heated. This blend of healing traditions was, to say the least, noteworthy. But I would bet that the doctor's warm and gentle tone, his slower pace, and his Indianness produced as much positive effect as his alternative treatments.

I might also mention here the best evidence I have on the protectiveness with which providers approach their work at Gila River. At the end of my fieldwork, in the course of making final reports to various people and offices in the community, I distributed copies of a written draft. From this, I intended to collect further data in the form of feedback, criticisms, and questions from both informants and providers. When this report caught the attention of the medical staff, I quickly learned an important lesson about the difference between academic and clinical writing. Peppered, albeit modestly, with distanced accusations of the "biomedical establishment" and its faceless minions, that unedited report drew the scathing and angry criticisms of three clinicians—particularly those who did not know me and my better intentions. It took several weeks of phone calls and office visits, and an address to the entire medical staff, to ease clinicians' concerns about my work.

The medical staff are, not surprisingly, keenly aware of the cultural differences that challenge clinicians' effectiveness and success, and they expressed gratitude for the ethnographic details I could offer. But in the words of one prenatal diabetes educator, to whom I remain grateful for political advice and steering through that crisis, I could "save the diatribe." It is an important distinction, the distinction between working clinicians and biomedical hegemony. Applied medical anthropologists ignore it at their peril.

Trends in Treatment and Treatments

I have mentioned some of the clinical heroes at Gila River, but there are thousands like them nationwide, equally dedicated to their patients and community. To put the provider's perspective in its national context, I have only to mention the more than 11 million people in the United States with diabetes and the nearly $100 billion spent annually on its resulting medical complications. In 1995 and in response to the growing prevalence of diabetes in the United States, the Health Care Financing Administration (now known as the Centers for Medicare and Medical Services) and the National Institute of Diabetes, Digestive and Kidney Disorders (NIDDKD) initiated a nationwide assessment of the quality of diabetes care. The resulting Diabetes Quality Improvement Project (DQIP) involved not only these national organizations but also the ADA, the American Academy of Family Practice, the American College of Physicians–American Society of Internal Medicine, the Centers for Disease Control and Prevention, and the Veterans Health Administration, among others. With this powerful and influential command center, the DQIP has had a very successful start, identifying and recognizing those centers that best meet the national standards for diabetes care. The nationwide effort has become better coordinated, and clinicians have access to the research, support, and guidance they need to better treat their patients with or at risk for diabetes (Fleming et al. 2001). The diabetes troops are among the best coordinated.

Another national effort exists in the U.S. Department of Health and Human Services' (2000) *Healthy People 2010* (HP2010) agenda. This publication is the second such report providing a national assessment of health and goals for the future decade. In the first report (HP2000), four diabetes objectives were addressed, including prevalance of the disease in the United States, mortality, complications, and patient education. Later, a fifth objective was added for screening of diabetic retinopathy. By 2010, diabetes becomes a focus area in the report and receives much greater attention both by itself and in its relationship to other HP2010 goals and focus areas. The number of objectives was expanded from five to seventeen, and for each objective further surveillance and data are occurring.

Professionals at Gila River and nationwide lament the increasing rates of diabetes and obesity with regularity. Nationally, it is the generalist or primary care physician who is responsible for most diabetes care. But primary care practice is often focused on acute care. The needs of patients with diabetes and other chronic diseases are quite different from those of the acute care population in terms of both treatment and education. Visits to primary care physicians typically involve more time spent on nutrition counseling, feedback on test results, health education, exercise, and health promotion, and on assessing the patient's compliance with a treatment plan. And compared to acute-care visits, diabetes patients typically spend more time in education and assessment and less time on procedures (Yawn et al. 2001). So primary care physicians are challenged to meet the demands—both in terms of time and in terms of how that time is spent—of this population.

HP2010 does not contain specific practice guidelines or program recommendations, but it does target providers of diabetes care for education on best practices, the ADA standards of care, and other national standards for diabetes management. Even so, provider education alone is insufficient for improving care in health centers.

In one New York City community health center, barriers to achieving these standards of quality included staff turnover, the difficulty of implementing new programs aimed at quality in a clinic with already major demands on its resources, and the need for intensive patient education (Chin et al. 2000). To expand the effort, many have called for a consideration of diabetes as a "public health concern." This nomenclature translates into a perspective that addresses important social, cultural, and environmental factors and consequences of disease.

Providers are even being called upon to get involved in the community of the patient, so they can "begin to address the social, cultural, and environmental issues of patients' lives" (Elder and Muench 2000). In the process, they might also impact other groups through primary prevention, affect public policy, lobby, and be a role model (Elder and Muench 2000). So expectations are rising that physicians do whatever is necessary to be effective with their patients.

Tailor the Message

Pimas want to avoid diabetes. They want to learn, but not always through the traditional, Western methods of written materials and lecture. They want to eat, they want to laugh, and they want to be talking. And it doesn't hurt if there's a door prize.

There are three types of diabetes prevention: primary, secondary, and tertiary. Primary prevention—prevention among people without disease or symptoms—is the best-known by Pima people, because these are the fun runs, the children's school activities, the high-profile/low-investment things. The degree to which these are effective is the million-dollar question at Gila River. But right now, families don't "advise" or "teach" each other, and health decisions are really individual decisions.

Secondary prevention—prevention among people with symptoms—receives the most attention at Gila River, because it is primarily at the moment of diagnosis that Pimas are instructed about prevention. But the required diet and exercise programs are difficult and often unpopular. People know that fat and salt and sugar should be limited, but the general consensus seems to be that "it's too much work for too little reward." They eat horrible food that they can't taste, because there's not enough salt, and they miss their favorite foods, all to drop a pound or two (from 350!) or lower their blood sugar 5 points (from 200!). What's the use, they say, when "I really feel just fine" or, at least, normal? And when "everyone around me is eating what they want to eat."

Tertiary prevention—prevention of complications among people with disease—is a little more straightforward, because people have clear symptoms and "get the connection." However, there are plenty of elders who say, "I'll never go on dialysis" or "I just don't want to have surgery" (e.g., for gangrene).

One of the greatest challenges for diabetes prevention and treatment among Native Americans is the need to resist overgeneralizing among tribes. Because of the breadth and intensity of the problem among Native Americans, there is a strong inclination (and practical need) to design pan-tribal messages about diabetes prevention and treatment in these groups. But discourse on Indian approaches to health is still peppered with ethnocentric oversimplifications. Some discussions of Indian identity have identified a pan-tribal approach to the future. Reid and Rhoades state, "Taking one day at a time, maintaining the hope that the next day may bring improvement, is the usual method of bearing an illness. Living one day at a time without thinking about the future is consistent with the tradition of many Indians of not planning for the future" (2000:420). This description of Indians' living without thought for the future may itself be short-sighted. Reid and Rhoades overgeneralize not only to all tribes but for all situations and contexts. Pimas, arguably all tribal members, do plan, but the planning is not in the form expected. Kozak's elaboration of Indians securing the future through work on relationships today may be a more meaningful explanation of the Pima approach to adversity.

The Department of Health and Human Services requires that health providers undergo regular education in cultural (and linguistic) sensitivity. Since the model programs for diabetes were instituted, community-based spin-off projects that strive for cultural sensitivity and relevance have started up all over Indian Country. These programs use, for example, cultural stories and metaphors for learning, may be offered in native languages, and are in other ways tailored to the local native population. Others devote enormous resources to personalized, supported care.[1]

Increasingly, attention is paid to local perceptions and beliefs about diabetes. Patient attitudes, health beliefs, threat appraisals, and emotional responses have all been examined as relevant to the management of this disease (Hampson et al. 1995). Using interviews and questionnaires, the personal model of illness is a clinical and research tool that identifies several dimensions in a patient's view of diabetes: identity (knowledge associated with the disease label), time line (beliefs about disease course), consequences or effects of the disease, causes of the disease (which assesses the degree of personal responsibility felt by the patient for his or her condition), and cure for acute diseases (Hampson et al. 1995). The theory of personal models suggests that patient responses on these elements can predict certain aspects of diabetes self-care. Two dimensions of the personal-model interview—patient perceptions concerning the helpfulness of treatment and satisfaction with medical care—are predictive of that patient's adherence to a plan for diet and physical activity. Although such lengthy interviews are rarely made a regular part of interviews, the existence of these types of instruments is indicative of the growing trend toward cultural sensitivity and psychosocially informed diabetes care.

A troublesome area for clinicians is eliciting reports of symptoms from patients. Evaneshko (1994) describes how differences in symptom perception between Indians and non-Indians can lead to problems in provider/patient communication that affect the timely diagnosis and treatment of diabetes. She finds that "the Navajo patient's apparent lack of preparation in presenting a series of symptoms may result in a general gloss rather than any one specific complaint" (ibid.: 366). This is comparable to Pima use of the phrase, perhaps a euphemistic device, "some way" to describe their current feelings and symptoms. It also helps explain some Pimas' reluctance to make appointments for minor symptomatic problems.

A good deal of energy is placed on educating Pimas about different food groups, the food "pyramid," the importance of fruits and vegetables, and how to prepare foods with less salt and fat. An analogy that educators sometimes use for this message is gas for the car. But there are lots of broken-down cars on the reservation. A specific problem in communication has been identified, however, which is the focus on avoidance of sugars and sweets as key to diabetes prevention, rather than the reduction of fats and carbohydrates. This problem is present to a degree in the more brief health education messages and is mirrored in Pima talk about healthy eating. Some Pimas who do not eat sweets such as candy and pop, but who eat daily diets high in fatty, salty, fried foods, including "fast foods" and home-cooked meals of *chumuth* and *wamuchtha*, are surprised to learn that they have diabetes.

At the same time, Pima narratives of diabetes etiology cannot be truncated into simplistic perceptions. Garro reveals:

> At first glance, it may appear that people do not fully understand the basic biomedical "information" about diabetes and that their accounts suggest the need for more and better educational material. Yet, . . . most people were well informed about the standard medical explanations for their illness and the basic instructions for its treatment, and they also continued to draw upon and to speculate about other kinds of knowledge regarding health and healing. . . . What is interesting and important about such statements, whether those of Dakota or of others, is that they are creative attempts that all laypersons express in their efforts to make sense out of their on-going life experience and the disruptions of it, experience that includes in this instance the symptoms of diabetes and the requirements of diabetes management. (1994: 321)

The analogy of gas in a car conjures images of weakness and a need for fuel to Pima women with whom I spoke about it. To "fuel" the body, a variety of old and young Pima women said that a "full meal" such as popovers or a burger was needed, and not a "snack" of an apple or carrot. The chosen analogy, thereby, becomes more problematic to those Pimas who interpret the symptoms of diabetes as requiring fuel. This is why Alice kept drinking 7-Up and apple juice to try to rehydrate herself during the flu. These drinks made her glucose level rise to a potentially life-threatening 900 mg/dl (80–180 mg/dl is considered normal depending on the recency of meals and time of day). The need to impart specific knowledge about appropriate foods, their effects on the body, and useful/harmful serving sizes has become clear as an essential part of health education.

The message about obesity and diabetes appears simple. There is a dose-response or direct relationship between physical activity and risk of diabetes (Wing 2001). But numerous environmental factors play a role in physical activity and eating:

- Obesity rates in people of lower socioeconomic status are influenced by their reduced access to affordable, healthy foods and opportunities for physical activity. (Hill and Peters 1998)
- Cheadle et al. (1995) documented a strong correlation between fat intake in a community and the amount of local grocery store shelf space devoted to low-fat versus regular milk and meat.
- The amount of exercise equipment in the home is associated with adult physical activity levels. (Jakicic et al. 1997)
- The physical activity level of children is related to the characteristics of their neighborhood, such as distance between homes and other environmental factors. (Sallis et al. 1990)
- Changing the signs to promote the use of stairs rather than elevators can have important effects. (Anderson et al. 1998; Brownell et al. 1980)
- Changing the food supply in schools, cafeterias, and vending machines influences both adults and children in their food purchases and physiological risk factors. (Ellison, Capper, and Stephenson 1989; Ellison, Capper, Goldberg, et al. 1989; French et al. 1997; Jeffery et al. 1994)

Thus, even simple messages become complex treatment issues. Despite epidemiological data that link diabetes with obesity, Pimas agree that any individual's chances are the same. Both "chunky" (a term Pimas use to describe people greater than about 200–250 lbs.) and thin Pimas get diabetes. Prevention messages that are focused on weight loss are not convincing to women, given this rule and their knowledge of incidence. Every woman had chunky friends and relatives that were not diabetic. These are the anecdotal cases that become prominent in women's minds and memories and have a big effect on their own sense of vulnerability to diabetes. These anecdotes need to become part of the clinical discussion, so that their impact on patient decisions can be assessed and, if possible, mediated.

The term *treatment* connotes a variety of meanings: a regimen of self-care and monitoring, medications, the way patients are "treated" by their providers. The diabetes epidemic is refusing to relent under standard practices in biomedicine. New theories of patient empowerment and support are stepping in to fill some of the gap. Thus, a single "treatment" cannot be identified for any diabetes patient or for any high-risk ethnic group. And all of these clinical efforts at producing individualized care yield good improvements in outcome.

But, as Tripp-Reimer et al. (2001) have discussed, diabetes programs that are culturally sensitive are now the most elementary form of intervention in Indian Country; only programs that aim for community-wide transformation will have an impact on diabetes prevalence. It is becoming even more important to respond with flexibility, sensitivity, and attentiveness to the modulations of Pima beliefs about health and diabetes (Hahn 1995; Loustaunau and Sobo 1997), especially as these vary in different generations or age groups. It is also becoming clear that energies dedicated to the clinical encounter—adding emphasis and responsibility to already overstretched providers—will not curb prevalence growth.

The clinical setting must be decentered as the primary site for diabetes education and prevention. If the epidemic is to be stemmed, either at Gila River or elsewhere in the industrial world, change must transform these communities.

8

Diagnostic Controversy

Gestational diabetes mellitus is a disease that powerfully demonstrates the heterogeneity of medicine. Not a "coherent whole . . . [but] an amalgam of thoughts, a mixture of habits, an assemblage of techniques," biomedicine and biomedical knowledge are formed out of human acts and interaction (Berg and Mol 1998:3). A discussion of the professional controversy over diagnosis of diabetes draws attention to its historical moment and to the research context that so drives diagnostic knowledge. On this point, Rapp has provided a particularly human and sharp perspective on the "problem of stabilization and disambiguation" of scientific decisions (Rapp 1999:208). In that ethnography, she explores many angles to the production of knowledge about amniocentesis and points out that "among insiders, the acknowledgment of ambiguity, uncertainty, and stabilizing judgment calls is part of normal and normalizing cytogenic practice" (Rapp 1999:209). A similar discourse now exists in professional circles about GDM diagnosis.

Since the 1980s, there has been quite a bit of disagreement within biomedicine over the diagnosis of GDM. Aspects of the controversy have included: the appropriateness of testing (Jarrett 1997), the methods by which testing should be done (Neiger and Coustan 1991; Juutinen et al. 2000; Neilson et al. 1991; Perucchini et al. 1999; Pettitt 2001; Weiss et al. 1998), the cutoff values for diagnosis (Corcoy et al. 2000; Magee et al. 1993; Neiger and Coustan 1991; Rust et al. 1996; B. Weiss et al. 1989), the costs of various methods (Bonomo et al. 1998; de Aguiar et al. 2001; Schwartz et al. 1999), and the need for different cutoff values for different ethnic groups (Green et al. 1990). In spite of all this research effort, the U.S. Preventive Services Task Force was unable, based on current evidence of benefits and harms of screening, to recommend for or against routine screening for gestational diabetes in the general population (U.S. Preventive Services Task Force 2003). Nor could they state which approaches to screening and diagnosis are optimal.

As David Pettitt stated in 2001, "the controversy over what screening test (if any) to use for the diagnosis of GDM and how to interpret the results is unlikely to be resolved quickly" (2001:1129). While the adoption of the 75-gram glucose load test by the ADA (based on the endorsement of the Fourth International Workshop–Conference on GDM) has since 1977 given clinical practice its direction and focus, the meaningfulness of the test remains in debate. At Gila River, where the entire population is deemed at high risk for diabetes, all pregnant women are tested for GDM at the first appointment or as early as possible.

The controversy among experts reveals important characteristics of the disease and tests for it that are likewise apparent to many patients, despite the sometimes authoritative presentation of the diagnosis and its screening devices by health care providers. Central to this discussion is the professional disagreement over the place or moment at which to make a diagnosis. And feeding the debate are questions about macrosomia (high birth weight) and other negative birth outcomes and the meaningfulness of population averages for certain high-prevalence ethnic groups (including the Pima).

The fact that a diagnostic controversy exists is evidence of the problematic boundary line between diabetic and nondiabetic. This line is drawn neatly by official American Diabetes Association thresholds, but the long-term impact of "high normal" glucose may be quite profound (Lao and Ho 2004; Mello et al. 2003; B. Weiss et al. 1989), so the boundary line is frequently questioned. In much of recent research, diagnostic criteria and methods are evaluated for their ability to predict negative birth outcomes such as high birth weight (Jarrett 1997; Mello et al. 2003; Neilson et al. 1991; Rust et al. 1996; Schmidt et al. 2001) *not* for their ability to predict future diabetes in the mother and infant (as in Dabelea et al. 2000; Lindsay et al. 2000; Pettitt et al. 1993). Speaking generally, the diagnosis of diabetes is not so much a measurement of current complications or symptoms as it is a statistically determined threshold for predicting future complications and outcomes. A patient's health status at the first diagnosable moment is quite good (though this is rarely when they're actually diagnosed); diabetes is much more often diagnosed late in the vascular destructive process. So conservatives wish to push the boundary line lower to capture more of those at risk for complications, and to catch them earlier.

Given that diabetes diagnostic criteria are strongly reflective of statistical associations (of later complications), it is appropriate to note the differences between ethnic groups of diabetes rates and complications. It is with these differences in mind that some researchers are calling for different diagnostic thresholds for different ethnic groups. Though it falls dangerously close to the slippery slope of racism in diagnosis, this recommendation has some merit. If the diagnostic threshold itself is already determined by statistical forecasting, then it seems appropriate to offer revised statistical forecasting for relevant, significant subpopulations. To insist that each subgroup (including ethnic groups like the Pima Indians) be treated using comparisons against a global (or national) norm is not only unnecessary, but unreasonable and unethical. Whether or not those revised diagnostic thresholds are made "official" by the ADA or other endorsement, I leave to those bodies to decide. But decisions are already being made at Gila River that respond to their greater-than-population-average risk for diabetes, including earlier testing for GDM and even a new diagnostic category of "pre-GDM" (which I will discuss later). There is, therefore, an interactional element to diabetes knowledge.

Pima women's words reflected an understanding of the GDM diagnosis as a work-in-progress rather than a clear and final diagnosis. Although biomedical definitions strictly contradict this understanding, GDM is by all counts a temporary form of the disease. Women whose glucose remains high after pregnancy must be *reclassified* as type 2 and do not retain the diagnosis of GDM.

In interviews and in less formal settings, Pima women expressed a good understanding of most of their prenatal tests, including such activities as fetal kick counts, electronic fetal monitoring (stress tests), and urine analyses for iron and other trace elements. The screening for gestational diabetes, however, has some complicated characteristics that germinate more creative interpretations. Namely, a positive screening for gestational diabetes may well be followed after birth by normal blood glucose readings. Both physicians and diabetes educators know and are careful to share information about this trait of GDM, and that women may expect to see their glucose return to normal; but this does not return women to their pre-GDM state of risk for developing type 2 diabetes. In contrast to biomedical understandings of this process, women explained the postbirth return to normal glucose as indicative of a mistaken or a premature diagnosis—not really diabetes. Similar fluctuations in test results, and the subsequent irregularity or inconsistency in the diagnostic message, have been discussed with regard to hypertension (e.g., Blumhagen 1980; Heurtin-Roberts 1993; Schoenberg 1997).

The view of GDM as a work in progress might dissuade women from completing referrals to the DEC until their diagnosis is more permanent or, in their opinion, certain. This interpretation, of course, can also be used to justify a delay in prevention behaviors that are so important in this population. It is not even safe to assume that a biomedical understanding of GDM will motivate behavioral change. Persily (1996) has shown that women who perceive GDM to have a great impact on their lives are less likely to make behavioral changes associated with glucose control.

The clinical or educational response to this dilemma has typically been to better inform women of the biomedical meaning of GDM versus type 2 diabetes and the nature of their relationship. What remains unaddressed, however, is the problematic notion of diabetes as a disease—as something greater than the sum of its complications. The health complications of diabetes are often foremost in the minds of Pimas. The amputations, blindness, and dialysis are what seem to them to characterize the diabetic's life.

Is a GDM diagnosis clear and reliable? Or does a GDM diagnosis contribute to prenatal stress in ways that would actually discourage women from following up on diabetes referrals, as was found by Persily (1996)? As I have discussed elsewhere (Smith-Morris 2004), the issues facing this population are complex, while the stakes—that is, the links between GDM and subsequent diabetes in mother and child —are high. Pima women's utilization of prenatal diabetes education is contingent upon their interpretation of the diagnostic process that, for GDM, seems to contradict subsequent normal blood glucose levels. This research reveals that women's interpretations of GDM are heavily influenced by the peculiar aspects of the disease (table 8.1). In short, women have identified and grapple with the *same* conceptual problems of GDM as diabetes professionals do.

At least two potential improvements in diabetes care and educa-

Table 8.1 Lay questions and biomedical explanations for diabetes

One might reasonably ask	Biomedical explanations (where consensus exists)
What's the difference between gestational diabetes and "regular" diabetes?	Diabetes is defined as having multiple forms, though the end result is the same in each form: high blood glucose.
How can it be diabetes if I don't feel bad?	Most visible, and thus foremost in the mental image of Pimas, are the complications of diabetes, including blindness, amputation, and the need for dialysis.
How can it be diabetes if it goes away?	The high blood glucose of gestational diabetes mellitus disappears after birth. If high blood glucose persists, then the woman must be reclassified as having type 2 diabetes.
If my test numbers are normal, how can I be diabetic?	Diagnosis of diabetes involves a numerical threshold that, once crossed (or crossed twice, depending on the test), permanently connotes the diagnosis. Later normal glucose levels, regardless of their duration, do not remove the diagnosis or warrant any kind of "in remission" status.

tion can be harnessed to facilitate these meaning negotiations in balanced and effective ways. First, privileging women's experiences in the diagnostic and educational dialogue not only will improve communication but will ultimately foster better compliance with diabetes management plans. Comprehensive conversations between provider and patient allow the provider a voice in the patient's translation of biomedical information into personally meaningful concepts. The longer and more deeply providers involve themselves in that process of translation, the more likely it will be that key biomedical concepts (e.g., weight loss, prenatal control of glucose) "take hold" in women's lives.

But the moment of diagnosis is a late start for diabetes education.

Alice told me she was not referred to diabetes education until her blood glucose reached life-threatening levels.[1]

> **Alice:** When I took that diabetes [test] again, I didn't take diabetic prevention. I took diabetic education after my sugar went to 900. Up to 900! And then I ended up on insulin. Then they gave me the diabetic education class, and I told them, I told them, they should've been given to me when I was first diagnosed with diabetes.

Some, of course, attend appointments but make few or no behavioral changes for diabetes prevention and management. Some skip the classes altogether. The alternative group appointments offered by one physician might be useful for prenatal care, during which diabetes education and awareness are so important.

It will be a continuing goal to identify thematic discrepancies between biomedical information presented in prenatal appointments or diabetes classes and what women perceive. This research addressed these discrepancies for the concepts of "risk" and "borderline" diabetes, but there are other elements in diabetes education that seem vulnerable to cultural reinterpretation, such as the accuracy and reliability of finger-stick glucose readings and, particularly for the Pima, what constitutes "exercise," "swelling," or "excessive thirst." Michielutte (1994) and others (e.g., Ferzacca 1990; Joe 1994; Lang 1990; Olson 1999; Rock 2003) are useful resources, in both content and methodology, for these types of questions. Much also rests on providers' ability to encourage women's enrollment in, completion of, and behavioral responses to diabetes education. The most effective strategy may be preconceptual services, including education and case management that would make diabetes lifestyle changes more attainable for Pima women.

The second improvement to be made in conjunction with these one-to-one strategies is the strengthening of community-based efforts at Gila River. In the interest of space, I will quickly list the most important of these. (A fuller discussion is in Smith-Morris 2004; and in Smith-Morris 2006.) (1) A population-based approach, which recognizes the high-risk status of this ethnic group without losing sight of the differences among Pimas in their risk behaviors, resources, and readiness for prevention is fundamental. (2) Diabetes education campaigns must be invigorated and expanded to target all Pimas, and especially all pregnant women, not just those with diagnosable forms of diabetes or prediabetes. Delaying education until after diagnostic confirmation of diabetes or prediabetic conditions is reckless. (3) Popular formats, such as the group education format and one provider's group appointments, should be used more widely, and resources should be employed to expand upon those good ideas. (4) Field nurses who spend time in patients' homes are also popular and should be used as a clinical model for these rural, dispersed populations. These nurses develop a closer relationship with their patients and encourage two-way communication about diabetes, thereby acknowledging the negotiated aspects of knowledge production around this disease. (5) Youth, and particularly youth just prior to sexual activity, should be a focus of prevention education. A diabetic pregnancy is profoundly dangerous to a fetus in the first several weeks of gestation. This is weeks before the first diabetes screening is usually conducted. As mentioned earlier, the intrauterine environment may have as much impact as genetics on the fetus's (eventual) development of diabetes. One influence is environmental, the other genetic, but both significantly impact the development of the metabolic system in humans. So Pimas must recognize their ability to prevent the future generations' diabetes in the earliest stages of pregnancy. To the credit of the community and many dedicated professionals at Gila River, there is a strong school-based initiative for diabetes education. There is a gap in education, however, for older teens and "20-something" adults: precisely the age groups starting families.

It produces in me no small ambivalence to draw attention to the experiences and interpretations of pregnant Pima women. Because of their roles—as pregnant women, as mothers, as family cooks, and grocery shoppers—women are at the bulls-eye for diabetes prevention efforts. But technologies have "potentials that are at once both emancipatory and socially controlling" (Rapp:155). While we may understand the genetic, political, economic, and cultural influences on diabetes among the Pima (Smith-Morris 2004), the impact of the intrauterine environment connects, inextricably, the Pima mother's behaviors and decisions with the future health of all Pimas. The temptation therefore grows to police pregnant Pima women for their contribution to intrauterine diabetes transmission and, thus, the epidemic.

A counterbalance to this slippery slope must exist in the privileging of women's interpretations and experience of pregnancy. It is not simply logistical barriers that prevent women from attending and participating in prenatal care and diabetes education (which *are* shown to improve both prenatal health and glucose control). It is also women's interpretations of the diagnostic process that affect their openness to educational messages. This ethnography demonstrates the ability of Pima women to question the same ambiguities of the GDM diagnostic process as are questioned by professionals. Their interpretations of risk insist on the inclusion of experiential information, as we have learned is true of so many populations speaking through medical ethnographies. Processes of knowledge production *can* be acknowledged and productively harnessed in clinical encounters. At Gila River, this is already being done to some extent in group appointments with physicians, group education classes, and the work of field nurses. These formats for education and treatment will prove their worth in the better attendance, adherence to treatment plans, verbal involvement of patients in plan development, and, ultimately, reduced blood glucose of their patients. Through these mechanisms, diagnostic controversy and the negotiated meaning of diabetes risk are harnessed as the very mechanisms by which diabetes can be prevented.

NOTE: Parts of this chapter were originally published as "Diagnostic Controversy: Gestational Diabetes and the Meaning of Risk for Pima Indian Women" in *Medical Anthropology* 24(2)(2005):145–177.

Part IV

9

Land and Water

The decline of farming set the stage for the diabetes epidemic in two ways. First, the need for alternative sources of food led—not inevitably but certainly—to subsequent reliance on government commodities and other processed foods. Second, increased sedentism was associated with the change in subsistence activities from farming to wage labor. No longer was strenuous activity a normal part of life; it would come to hold a separate cultural nomenclature called "exercise." Both of these factors are entangled now with notions of Pima culture.

The Pimas' skills for desert farming and efficient irrigation practices were time-tested. There is archaeological evidence of Hohokam irrigation farming dating as far back as AD 800 (Castetter and Bell 1942:28). Even in drought years, Pimas survived by seeding multiple fields in hopes that at least one would obtain enough water to produce. At least maize and two types of beans were in cultivation during the Hohokam period (AD 1000) as well as when the Pimas were first encountered by a European, Father Eusebio Kino in 1687 (Ortiz 1973). Through contact with the Spanish, Pimas began growing wheat (a winter crop) and raising cattle in addition to their farming, hunting, and gathering. But land and water would become increasingly precious resources in what is now a familiar story of colonization and cultural domination.

From early colonial history into the middle of the twentieth century, the American legal system based its dealings with Indians on the doctrine of discovery, which set a legal relationship between European discoverers and the Indian tribes (see Deloria and Lytle 1984:4; Shattuck and Norgren 1991:110). Based on this principle, treaties with Indians respected Indians' rights of land occupancy and possession and their right to extinguish Indian title by consenting to it in writing.

Treaties between the federal government and Indian nations, rather than state land grants and contracts with Indians, were also chosen as a national policy, thus to some degree standardizing the process and recognizing Indian tribes as nations. But competition over land led quickly to the misuse of treaties and an unbearable burden on the federal government until, in 1871, legislation was passed to ban all new treaties. Justice John Marshall's use of the doctrine of discovery, also known as the last-in-time rule, created a precedent that allowed Indian treaties to be overridden by subsequent congressional action. "Tribal nations . . . were no longer recognized as polities capable of treating with the United States, yet they remained separate if wholly unequal sovereigns, outside the pale of the American Constitution" (Deloria and Lytle 1984).

The Spanish government had claimed official control of the Southwest from the sixteenth century until the Mexican Revolution of 1821. The Treaty of Guadalupe Hidalgo, signed in 1848, would shift part of this territory from Mexican to U.S. control. And in 1853, with the Gadsden Purchase, the remaining area, including the area of the present-day Gila River Indian Reservation, would become U.S. territory. Arizona was organized as a territory in 1861, though statehood came several decades later. This was a period of great land competition and highly political boundary negotiations. In 1830, hundreds of thousands of Native Americans were forcibly relocated to forts and reservations in Florida and Oklahoma. Other tribes, such as the Pima, remained on small reservations, dependent for their survival on handouts from the federal government because their means of subsistence had been stolen or destroyed. The Supreme Court under Justice Marshall conceived of the doctrine of discovery and named tribes "domestic dependent nations," their relation to the United States "resembl[ing] that of wards to a guardian" (30 US 1, 1823). These concepts remain fundamental today in the legal relationship between the federal government and Native Americans.

The relevance of history to modern rates of diabetes in the Pima has to do in large part with their forced transition from subsistence farming to a wage economy.[1] This transition began when the Pimas "learned" that any excess crops could be sold or bartered for Spanish imports such as iron tools, guns, cloth, sugar, and alcohol (Castetter and Bell 1942:39). After the mid-1800s, many Indians became accustomed to and later dependent on the goods available through trade and sale (Wolf 1982). Pressure from white migration increased until 1859, when the Gila River Indian Reservation was created (Bahti and Bahti 1997).

Viewed originally as a mechanism for creating physical distance between Indians and non-Indians, reservations came to be seen as a way to "civilize" Indians through the work of missionaries and the supervision of an Indian agent. After treaty making came to an end in 1871, off-reservation boarding schools were established to permit the education of Indian children away from their tribal environments (1878). A Court of Indian Offenses, with judges appointed by the Indian agents, was established to further the civilizing mission of the reservations, and certain religious dances and customary practices were outlawed.

Two late-nineteenth-century events dealt profound changes to the Southwestern tribes: the railroads, which flooded the Southwest with goods, tourists, and migrants; and the General Allotment Act (or "Dawes Act") of 1887. This act authorized the president to allot portions of land to individual Indians.[2] After receiving allotments, the allottees became U.S. citizens. But all "excess" Indian lands, that is, all acreage not distributed in individual allotments, were retained by the federal government for non-Indian settlement. Through this process, Indian-held land dropped from 138 million acres in 1887 to 50 million acres in 1934 (Hauptman 1994).

By the late nineteenth century, almost all of the Pima farms had dried up due to the loss of water to upstream whites who violated "prior appropriation" rights to the Gila River water flow (see Kelsey v. McAteer 1879 as described in Dobyns 1989). By 1895, the Pima, who had sold approximately 3 million bushels of surplus wheat to the U.S. Army and settlers only 25 years prior, had to be issued government rations (Bahti and Bahti 1997). President Theodore Roosevelt's policies, including the 1902 Federal Reclamation Act, began to transform the West into a more thoroughly colonized and exploited area. The 1903 Roosevelt Dam, for example, created ongoing problems of water and land access for the Navajos for farming and shepherding. During and after the "Forty Years of Famine" between 1871 and 1910, the Pimas struggled to survive (Ortiz 1973).

It was 1924 before a remedy for the drought came. The San Carlos Irrigation Project (SCIP) dammed the Gila River and dispersed the waters to both tribal and other area farms (Weaver 1973). Located in

Coolidge, the SCIP is a joint Indian and non-Indian project for irrigating 100,000 acres, of which 50,000 are Indian lands in the reservation and 50,000 are private or public non-Indian lands around the southern edge of the reservation. It took until the mid-1930s to complete the SCIP, though its water allocations proved to be unequal, leaving the Pimas only a partial water supply (Historic America Engineering Record 1996).

These events occurred in what was called the Indian Reorganization Period (1934–1952), when public sentiment deemed that "the tribes not only would be in existence for an indefinite period, but that they should be" (Canby 1988: 23). The 1928 Meriam Report documented the failure of allotment policies and heralded the Indian Reorganization Act, which authorized the secretary of the interior to acquire land and water rights and to set up reservations. Reservation employment levels remained low throughout the 1950s.[3] But in the period from 1953 to 1967, public sentiment and federal policy again shifted. Several tribes were terminated, and the status of Indians as wards of the United States was ended. The Bureau of Indian Affairs encouraged tribes to leave their reservations under relocation programs. Agricultural production had become regionally specialized and mechanized throughout the United States. Small-scale farmers could neither compete with neighboring monocroppers nor afford to reject the more efficient division of labor necessitated by industrialized, mechanized, mass-producing, capitalist society (Hackenberg 1955b: 162). The Pima could no longer support themselves through small-scale family farming. Larger, more productive and lucrative farming was necessary, as was eventually wage labor, income from leased lands, and federal aid money. Hackenberg states, "For fifty years, the [Pima] Indians had been gradually drawn more and more into a cash economy, first through being driven into wage work by the diminishing agricultural potential of the reservation during the dry years, and second through learning to depend on manufactured and processed goods produced off the reservation" (Hackenberg 1955a:89).

The Pimas were poorly prepared for the larger-scaled, more independent farming demanded by the Indian Bureau Extension Service's "reclamation program" (Hackenberg 1955a:83). Small family plots belonging to farmers who were neither well organized nor economically capable of harvesting enough to subsist upon were sold or leased to white farmers. Hackenberg explains that "credit and implements [for farming] were never provided for [the Pima] in anything like adequate amounts, and their acquaintance with project irrigation methods [was] scant" (1955a:86). Unlike Anglo farmers, Pimas were unable to obtain credit for conducting farm operations, leading to large differences in total crop values between these two groups (Pfaff 1994:65). Because family plots were scattered, often separated by plots leased to whites, "the majority of [Pima) families . . . [could] not form cooperative labor groups, nor [could] they pool their resources to purchase implements and other essentials" (Hackenberg 1955b: 148). Pima farmers had to rent equipment to perform necessary mechanical operations on the farm, and they relied on irrigation district water schedules that were not in their control. The SCIP was largely considered a failure, until very recently, due to inadequate supplies and the need for increasing numbers of wells. Pima farmers therefore chose their crops carefully, lest human-made circumstances beyond their control damage their season's profits. These circumstances, argues Hackenberg, explain why the Pima farmer could never become "self-sufficient" as governmental (and tribal) ideologies proclaimed. Instead, Pima farmers had to rely on part-time wage work, income from leased lands, and other sources of federal aid to make a living.

A significant break in the momentum of cultural and economic assimilation came in 1966 when the Pima gained control of community development. The focus for Gila River Indian Reservation development changed to promote education and training for industrial employment, and to create jobs for Indians on or near the reservation. Due in part to the continuing difficulties in adequate and cost-effective irrigation, other development opportunities have been explored for the Gila River Indian Reservation. This reservation was considered advantageous for noxious and hazardous industrial works because it is remote yet has good highway access (Western Management Consultants, Inc. 1963). Capital improvement planning contributes to coordinated efforts between the community, the Bureau of Indian Affairs, and other federal agencies, including the Farmers Home Administration and the Department of Housing and Urban Development (Simon Eisner and Associates 1973).

The Self-Determination Act of 1974 could not have worked without tribes having the capacity to administer their own affairs, a capacity that grew only during the prior 10–15 years. In 1968, President Johnson sent a message to Congress articulating his support for Indian self-determination and, through his "War on Poverty," created programs on reservations that would build Indian skills and self-governance capacity. The War on Poverty built tribal capacity, because it was the first time tribes themselves were given the money to try—and were allowed to succeed or fail. One of the most important economic changes for tribes has been the rejection of the grant concept of support from the federal government in favor of contract-based support. A public law (PL 93-638) was passed to, effectively, take many programs away from the Bureau of Indian Affairs while maintaining U.S. legal and moral support for these services (e.g., health, education, etc.). This meant moving much responsibility and control for tribal health services away from the Indian Health Service (IHS) to the tribes. Under PL 93-638, many tribes do write "contracts" for BIA funds, allowing them more freedom to design and administer tribal programs. But, of course, tribal funds are therefore always vulnerable to political attitudes and the changing federal priorities of each new administration.

Farming is not particularly lucrative, is difficult work (especially in the Sonoran Desert), and requires substantial start-up investment. For these and other reasons, only a few Pimas are still farmers. Furthermore, in recent decades, farmers in this area primarily grew cotton and alfalfa. The Gila River Farm also produces olives and citrus for sale, but very little farm produce is sold in the community. The majority of community members, therefore, maintain little cognitive connection to farming or to the source of their foods, a cultural change that not only underlines many Pimas' reliance on grocery-store and commodity foods, but also undermines the growing of gardens. The Gila River Farms and irrigation offices are working to bolster farm production as recent water allotments have been corrected upward. Additionally, it would be beneficial for Pimas to grow, consume, and share or sell a wider variety of foods, including beans, squash, and other vegetables. It remains to be seen if and how this will impact the diet of average community members. Continued and even further tribal council and Health Care Corporation initiatives are needed for programs and events that encourage community awareness of, if not participation in, the Gila River Farms. These directions are common topics among tribal council and Farm Board members.

As Jackson (1994) and others have explained, the relationship between tribes and their cultures of food are a result of their millennia-long direct relationship to the land. Processed foods, made available first through government rations and later in the "fast food" market, have had a highly negative and steadily worsening impact on Pima health. The circulation of many food commodities new to the Pima, such as high-fat and high-salt content snacks and high-sugar drinks, also effected change in Pima diets. These new commodities were brought not only by merchants but especially in the form of federal food supplements to Indian reservations (Jackson 1994; Wilson et al. 1994). Also, it has been suggested that Pima men serving with the U.S. forces during World War II developed a preference for Western foods (Smith et al. 1994:415–416). Smith et al. describe a variety of foods that reflect a Mexican influence common in the Southwest: chili beans, chorizo sausage, corned beef and gravy or potatoes, ground beef and gravy, macaroni or chili, menudo, refried beans, tacos, tamales, and enchiladas. Unfortunately, "traditional" foods from before federal commodity days, such as tepary beans, are eaten only by a few Pimas. Yet Nabhan (Nabhan 1992; Nabhan et al. 1985) argues that tepary beans may even ameliorate diabetes problems through their slow digestion and lower insulin-raising properties.

In several 24-hour recall inventories of food intake that I conducted, I obtained a useful profile of Pima women's diets. There are several strengths and weaknesses of this method (Buzzard 1998). The strength of this method is that it accommodated any food or food combination reported, allowing women to describe "meals" in a way that was meaningful for them. This method also did not require women to read and complete a written form, a method that was determined to be difficult or uncomfortable for many participants during the pilot study phase of the work. However, since I did not observe these meals, I cannot validate these data, particularly the reported quantities. Even so, I was not so much interested in exact portions as in reasonable estimations. I suggested the use of my fist as a measuring device for portion sizes (one fist being a "serving" or "small bowl" size). A sample of these data appears in table 9.1 and does a good job of characterizing the diets of the participating women.

These data characterize women's diets as heavy in protein, carbohydrates, and fat, which corresponds with clinical literature on this subject. Having eaten a salad was rarely reported, and corn, beans, and potatoes were the only vegetables reported by these five women. (A total of eighteen such recall surveys were taken with a handful of

Table 9.1 Sample of 24-hour recall food inventories (approximate amounts)

	Nancy	Belle	Catherine	Tricia	Anne
Tea (oz)			8		16
Milk (oz)		16 (chocolate)		24	
Soda (oz)	68		40		
Kool-Aid (oz)				8	
Water (oz)	32		8	12	8
Cereal w/milk (bowl)	1	1	1	2	
Eggs	2	1		3	
Bacon/sausage	6			3	
Toast w/butter	6	4	2		
Fruit/juice	1	2	2		1
Tacos	4				
Fry bread			2		
Beans	2		2	2	
Chumuth (fried ground beef)				1	1
Cheese	1		2		
Rice	2				
Macaroni and cheese		1			
Corn				2	
Hot dog		1			
Hamburger				2	
Pork chop			1		
Grilled cheese sandwich					2
French fries			1		
Salad			1		
Chips	2	2			1
Candy bar				1	

other vegetables being reported.) Importantly, these vegetables are high-carbohydrate vegetables and are "counted" in the breads category by the ADA.

A rise in Pimas' dietary intake of fat from 15 percent in the 1890s to 40 percent in the 1990s is another important condition in the high rate of diabetes in this community (National Institute of Diabetes and Digestive and Kidney Diseases [NIDDKD] 1996:19). Approximately 95 percent of Pima Indians with diabetes are overweight (NIDDKD:16). Foods from federal and state-administered distribution programs include: eggs, bacon, potatoes, lard, cheese, beans, canned meats, vegetables and fruits, dry cereals, and dried or evaporated milk. Recent research has not provided definitive evidence indicating that the adoption of an Anglo diet increases the risk of developing diabetes in Pimas (Price et al. 1993; D. E. Williams et al. 2001); however, it is widely accepted that the traditional lifestyle of hunter-gatherer-horticulturalists would have protected against it (Jackson 1994).

Increased sedentism and high-fat/high-carbohydrate diets are characteristic of many Americans' lives. So these factors alone cannot explain the high rates of diabetes in the Pima. Several factors have converged to create this diabetic in the Pima.

Several theories on the etiology of diabetes in Native Americans have been debated (see Benyshek et al. 2001; Shapiro 1997). James Neel provided seminal work that described a "thrifty" genotype suited to the feast-or-famine conditions of early hunter-gatherer existence, either through a "quick insulin trigger," fewer receptor cells for glucose, or enhanced fat metabolism (1962, 1982). Wendorf and Goldfine (Wendorf 1989; Wendorf and Goldfine 1991) further argue that a lack of food resources encouraged increased mobility among Paleoindians, for whom kill sites became short-term camps. This argument means that a thrifty gene had already evolved as a physical adaptation to food scarcity (or unreliability) in eastern Beringia. However, this "thrifty" genotype hypothesis is not considered to be a sufficient explanation for the post–World War II rise in diabetes prevalence among the Pimas and other Native American groups (Knowler et al. 1990:9; Neel 1962). As Scheder (1988) found among mobile Mexican laborers, acculturative stress may also have played a role in Pima weight gain and increased incidence of hypertension, two factors comorbid with diabetes.

Prehistoric environmental changes, including dietary change, are critical components of the diabetes profile of Pimas (Knowler et al. 1983; Knowler et al. 1990; Ravussin et al. 1994; Weiss 1985). Szathmary (1993) found that early hunters who efficiently metabolized fat in a carbohydrate-poor environment were more adaptive. But these adaptations, when present in individuals exposed to modern high-carbohydrate, low-protein diets, are more likely to lead to type 2 diabetes. The "New World syndrome" is posed as another explanation (K. Weiss et al. 1989) for type 2 diabetes insofar as it is one of a number of problems associated with dramatic environmental change resulting from colonial events in the New World. These problems include: obesity, gallbladder disease, and some digestive system cancers.

This combination of economic and genetic factors can be compared to some other Native American groups. For example, Wiedman has described how "ethnographic, historic and archeologic evidence documented the Cherokee's rapid cultural change from an agricultural to an industrial economy in a matter of ten years, from 1936 to 1946. This infrastructural change resulted in nutritional and lifestyle changes which contributed to obesity and the onset of detrimental diabetic symptoms" (Weidman 1987). Medical anthropologists have even begun to disentangle, where possible, the relationship between the economic environment and its genetic and biological ramifications.

In an article focused on the complexity of diabetes etiology, Benyshek et al. (2001) point out that two important problems exist with the hypothesis of a genetic basis for type 2 diabetes. First, there is little evidence that early hunter-gatherers experienced the periodic starvation that would favor an insulin-resistant gene. Second, some of the groups with the highest rates of diabetes (e.g., the Pimas, Puebloans, and River Yumans) also have the longest history of intensive agricultural subsistence. For this and several reasons elaborated by them, Benyshek et al. suggest that diabetes is an "acquired characteristic" beginning in utero (Benyshek et al. 2001:35). Their fetal origins model outlines two phases in the emergence of type 2 diabetes: first, a thrifty phenotype generation experiences severe famine conditions in utero and goes to develop abnormal insulin-glucose metabolism (especially when obese) in adulthood; and second, the subsequent generation(s), who, while not experiencing severe food shortage, develop hyperinsulinemia, insulin resistance, and eventually glucose intolerance in adult life as a result of excess fuels supplied to them in utero by glucose-intolerant mothers (Freinkel 1980). And I have already discussed research that confirms (1) mothers more than fathers transmit diabetes to their children and (2) mothers who had diabetes during pregnancy transmit diabetes more frequently than mothers who did not have diabetes during pregnancy.

Cultural factors in the prevalence of diabetes at Gila River have mainly to do with foodways, although other relevant cultural characteristics include styles of communication, attitudes about disease prevention, and practices related to personal autonomy and advice giving. Traditional foods such as beans and, more recently, fry bread are

Figure 9.1. Many Pima women take seriously their roles and obligations as good cooks.

pervasive at (and symbolic of) social, religious, and even work-related gatherings. Pima cooks take great pride in their fry bread and are generous with a variety of other fried and sweet foods (fig. 9.1). To please one's guests and family with food is the centerpiece of good host/essing and is quintessentially "the Pima way." The serving of food to visitors is a common and "serious obligation" among many Native American groups (Jackson 1994:381), while declining food that is offered can be a significant social error (Lang 1989). Take for example the Mexican American informant of Larme and Pugh who said, "I turned down my mother's tamales, and hurt her feelings, but my glucose didn't go down" (Larme and Pugh 2001:660). The gains in weight resulting from all this hospitality also make their way into cultural assumptions—for example, Hagey (1989:26) reported that thinness could be considered a sign of weakness or of poverty.

In all cultures, diet can be "a way to reestablish or break ties with tradition in a rapidly changing world" (Nichter 1980). In the case of the Pima, who have experienced some of the greatest acculturative pressures of all the Southwest tribes due to their length and form of contact with Europeans, definitions of "Indianness" are drawn from historical and environmental contexts that include a political economy of health. "Diseases of development," such as diabetes, obesity, and alcoholism, are recognized by Pimas to be "white man's diseases" (Joe 1994; Lipsman 1988), somehow attributable to white contact or influence. Yet Pimas recognize diabetes to be a pervasive problem in their community and, therefore, a particularly Piman problem. Diabetes thus symbolizes the experience of culture contact for Pimas.

Clearly, a strict attempt to unify traditionalism with dietary practice is increasingly irrelevant and impossible. Changing foods on the reservation, just like changing clothes, language, and healing practices, is not a "loss" of culture. Indeed, due to these changes being inextricable from the colonial process of domination and forced change, these new cultural features have an element of co-opted power.[4] Gretchen Lang, speaking about the Dakota, makes the point this way:

> While it may appear to be an ironic contradiction that there is reluctance to change food habits, given the commonly expressed idea that "white man's foods have made us sick," foods and foodways constitute complex codes for social relations and symbols of cultural identity. Many contemporary preferred foods, while incorporated into a traditional food system . . . are also recognized to have entered Dakota culture relatively recently, during a period recalled as one of great deprivation. Diabetes, especially as it affects food patterns, from an outsider's viewpoint appears to have provided the Dakota with another means through which to reflect and comment upon matters of continual concern regarding their history and their place with respect to the majority of society. (Lang 1990:309)

As the fairly recent addition of fry bread to the Pima's diet reveals, cultures are highly adaptive, and what is "traditional" need not be limited by abstract notions of historic ideas (Wiedman 2001).

When important cultural symbols (e.g., the eating of fry bread) are in conflict with biomedical messages about healthy behavior, creative programming is required to construct symbolic bridges between the relevant value systems (fig. 9.2). Altering dietary habits in slow increments has been the goal of many nutritionists' messages at Gila River. First, certain foods may be associated with affluence or comfort

Figure 9.2. The ubiquitous and celebrated fry bread, made from flour, salt, lard, baking soda, powdered milk, and water, then fried.

and therefore would be particularly valued by hosts and guests alike. These foods can increase the symbolic importance of an event and may improve a host's status. These food habits are less likely to change, so ancillary foods become the focus for fat and starch reduction. Second, foods that are associated (either truly or fictively) with the past, tradition, or Pima authenticity carry great symbolic value. Arguments about the nutritional content of such foods (e.g., fry bread) are difficult to make, since it is *not* for nutrition's sake that these foods are so carefully prepared, served, and consumed. Other cultural characteristics particularly important for diabetes programs to address include: the cost of food available on the reservation; limited access to transportation to hospitals and clinics; communicative patterns that make the transmission of sensitive or personal information in short (ten-minute) appointments difficult or impossible; and notions of authority and respectful behavior, including limited eye contact, not questioning directives or advice, and providing answers one thinks are wanted or expected, rather than answers from one's own opinion and knowledge. In many Native American communities, leaders and supervisors may be more highly valued and respected for advising, rather than ordering, those in their charge.[5]

Cultural factors, which are certainly important and have benefited many of the participants in programs previously described, can only help guide the disease reduction effort—they will not, alone, define it. Ethnographic data help inform tribal policy and diabetes program directors by helping to identify local priorities as well as to determine the most appropriate and culturally meaningful methods and processes for Pima goals to be reached. Cultural traits, oral histories, traditional practices, material culture, and history should be part of planning that molds and defines the community's future.

Several researchers have worked within the Gila River Indian Community on the problem of diabetes. The National Institutes of Health longitudinal diabetes research in this community has been of critical importance to the fight against diabetes worldwide.[6] Ritenbaugh's 1974 dissertation gives a broad view of the factors associated with diabetes among the Pima, including discussions of the early genetic findings produced by the National Institute of Diabetes, Digestive and Kidney Disorders. Ritenbaugh's dissertation does not include Pima narratives—that is, recorded interviews with Pimas' own words—and Ritenbaugh calls on others to "gain more information on the life histories of selected individuals in various [health] categories" (1974:111). My work is the first to focus on Pima narratives.

Three realms impacting the diabetes epidemic can be distinguished: cultural, genetic, and political-economic-historical. My ethnographic work with pregnant women revealed mostly cultural conflicts behind prevention and treatment adherence, particularly conceptual disagreements between biomedical and Pima conceptions of risk and the meaning and impact of diabetes screening during pregnancy. Of the major conceptual issues I identified, the concept of "exercise for exercise' sake" as foreign or impractical for some community members has already been mentioned.

A second area of disagreement stems from Western, biomedical notions of individual responsibility for health that are not universally accepted or even practical in the Pimas' kin-focused society. Kinship is still very important as a subsistence resource (and, for some, as a subsistence strategy in and of itself). Kin relationships impact one's income, access to food and transportation, and many other resources that determine a patient's ability to follow a diabetes treatment program. Pimas who remain this dependent upon and connected to kin networks will have a fairly consistent problem with treatment plans that assume individual responsibility for disease prevention and treatment. While community members have adopted many aspects of Anglo culture (e.g., the English language, Western-style clothing), and while the intent of biomedical providers is certainly altruistic, concepts of individuality and responsibility are being promoted as the best, if not only, way to achieve good health. It may be productive to view the educational events in which these concepts are taught as moments of culture contact. In this perceptual light, local ideas can be given greater weight, regardless of the nontraditional appearance of the people involved.

The genetic risk for diabetes associated with certain ethnicities, including Pima ethnic identity, are clearly relevant to the epidemic. Yet treatment and prevention of diabetes are challenging clinical problems in any population, especially where poor compliance with treatment regimens has been well documented (Beckles et al. 1998; Broussard et al. 1982; Narayan et al. 1998). Benyshek et al. (2001) suggest that genetically focused researchers have ignored or downplayed the nongenetic influences in Native American diabetes rates. Such "monocausal etiological model(s)" (Benyshek et al. 2001) have to a large degree permeated ideas about diabetes etiology among the Pima and may, thereby, foster "surrendered" attitudes (Kozak 1997) toward prevention and self-care. If programs and interventions are to be successful, this monocausal perspective must give way to a simultaneous understanding of the many factors, including political-economic and cultural factors, influencing diabetes rates in Native American communities.

Genetic factors complicate the task of diabetes prevention by (falsely) implying that the disease is unavoidable for Pimas. Instead, recent generations of undernourishment and stress during pregnancy have turned a genetic predisposition into a modern dilemma of catastrophic proportions. The critical problem with regard to genetic etiology is that perceptions of diabetes as inevitable can become self-fulfilling prophecies. To address the genetic factors, both small and large, formal and informal programs of change must be in place and in constant adjustment to the identified needs.

The task facing Gila River and its clinicians is how to blend the genetic, historical, and cultural aspects of diabetes into a single, coherent prevention strategy. The only place I have seen these three themes successfully blended is in the Pima identity itself.

Diabetes in America

Diabetes in America is a reflection of global processes of development, mass production, technologization, and homogenization. The 1997 estimate of global diabetes by Amos et al. was 124 million, or about 2.1 percent of the world population. This broke down to:

- 1 million in Oceania
- 8 million in Africa
- 13 million in North America
- 13 million in Latin America
- 22 million in Europe
- 66 million in Asia

In 2000, the International Diabetes Federation estimated there to be 151 million adults worldwide with the disease, increasing more than fivefold from 1985 (International Diabetes Federation [IDF] 2001). By 2010, the estimated total is projected to reach 221 million worldwide, with the fastest growth among Asian and African populations (see table 10.1). This will represent over 3.0 percent of the world's population. Diabetes is one of the top five leading causes of death in most developed countries (Amos et al. 1997).

About 85–90 percent of diabetes in developed countries, and virtually all diabetes in developing countries, is type 2 diabetes. Type 2 diabetes is usually diagnosed after the age of 40, although the age of onset is often earlier in contexts of economic development, where it is also often associated with obesity (Amos et al. 1997). The age-standardized rates for ages 30–64 vary dramatically: from less than 2 percent among rural Bantu in Tanzania to the 40–50 percent rate shared by the Pima and the Nauru in Micronesia. It is worth mentioning that diabetes was virtually unknown among the Nauru 50 years ago.

Table 10.1 Regional diabetes rates (in thousands)

Region	1995 population	1995 rate	2000 rate	2010 rate
World	5,697,038	118,417	151,227	220,718
Africa	731,470	7,294	9,412	14,152
Asia	3,437,786	62,782	84,510	132,297
North America	296,517	12,977	14,193	17,535
Latin America	475,704	12,403	15,566	22,541
Europe	727,787	22,040	26,507	32,865
Oceania	27,774	921	1,039	1,328

Source: Amos 1997

The prevalence of type 2 diabetes in developing countries is expected to increase dramatically in the next 25 years, particularly among Asian and Pacific Islander populations (IDF 2001). One in every five Native Americans is affected by diabetes, with rapid increases being recorded in the number of Native American children with the diagnosis (Lieberman 2004). The principal factor in this increase has been obesity, but it is closely followed by the effects of intrauterine exposure to high circulating glucose levels (Gohdes and Acton 2000).

Rising rates of diabetes will produce a worsening burden of health complications, particularly so because of the increasing longevity in humans and the changing demographic age distribution around the world (i.e., a larger elderly population). Amos et al. summarize: "With the unrestrained forces of economic globalization and industrialization, the prevalence of diabetes is likely to dramatically increase in the next millennium. The corresponding burden of complications and premature mortality resulting from diabetes will constitute a major public health problem for most countries" (Amos et al. 1997:S15). So while we can thank biomedical and technological advancements for giving us longer life, other characteristics of our time counteract some of that advantage, contributing to a sometimes painful and disabled period of old age.

10.4 Million

In 1998, an estimated 10.4 million people in the United States had diabetes. This number represents an increase of 2.9 million since 1980 (Geiss 1999). Trend watchers observed the increase: a 16 percent jump from 1980 to 1994; a 33 percent increase from 1990 to 1998 (Mokdad et al. 2000). Year 2010 estimates are at 11 million (prevalence of 4.0 percent), and at 29 million for the year 2050 (prevalence of 7.2 percent) (Boyle et al. 2001).

Such jumps—not just in the number of diabetes cases but in the rate at which new cases are diagnosed—foretell massive growth in diabetes prevalence in the United States. Boyle's projection also assumes a linear increase in prevalence, which understates the trends of the past two decades. The increase may actually be much higher.

Diabetes rates vary across subgroups of our population. Take, for example, the elderly, among whom half of the future increase will occur; that is, the prevalence of diabetes in those aged 65 and older rose from 8 to 10 percent in the 1970s and 1980s (Harris 1998), and to ~13 percent in the 1990s (Mokdad et al. 2000). But changing demographic factors in the United States will account for another substantial portion of our rising diabetes prevalence. Hefty growth projections point to the increasing prevalence of diabetes in childhood (Fagot-Campagna et al. 2000), and the largest increase in newly diagnosed diabetes occurring among individuals in their thirties (IDEA Health & Fitness Assn. 2001). Estimated prevalence of diabetes for adolescents age 12–19 (1988 and 1994) was 0.41 percent, although the study producing this data did not have a large sample of adolescents (Fagot-Campagna et al. 2001). Better data are certainly available for Native American adolescents: prevalence rates are estimated for Cree and Ojibway girls aged 10–19 to be 3.6 percent (Dean et al. 1998) and for Pimas aged 15–19 to be 5 percent (Dabelea et al. 1998). This prevalence rate for Pimas is a sixfold increase in two decades (Fagot-Campagna et al. 2001). So several age groups are seeing rate increases.

Significant differences exist in the diabetes rates among other groups of Americans. The ADA attributed 60 percent of the diabetes prevalence increase in the 1990s to Latinos: persons with Mexican American (60 percent of U.S. minorities), Puerto Rican (12 percent), Cuban (6 percent), and other Central and South American heritage (Lieberman 2004). Between 1988 and 1994, diabetes rates for non-

Hispanic blacks were 1.6 times the rate for non-Hispanic whites; the rates for Mexican Americans was 1.9 times the rate for non-Hispanic whites (Harris et al. 1998). An increasing proportion of blacks (from 12.8 percent in 2000 to ~14.7 percent in 2050) and other ethnicities (from 5.0 percent in 2000 to ~10.4 percent in 2050), and a reduction in the proportion of whites (from 82.2 percent in 2000 to ~74.9 percent in 2050) will also impact our national statistics (Boyle et al. 2001; Day 1996), leaving the nation with an enormous public health epidemic and health-care expenses to match.

Between 1990 and 1998, diabetes prevalence for Native American and Alaska native children and adolescents rose by 46 percent, more than three times the rate of increase in the U.S. general population (Acton et al. 2002). That many of these people are childbearing women presents additional public health concerns: fetal/child morbidity and mortality related to high blood glucose in the mother; maternal morbidity and complications of childbirth; increased prevalence of maternal type 2 diabetes after a diabetic pregnancy; and diabetes onset at a young age in the offspring of diabetic pregnancies (Acton et al. 2002). Evidence points to a worsening cycle in which Pimas are diagnosed with diabetes at a younger and younger age, impacting the pregnancies of even very young mothers. The younger age at onset of type 2 diabetes is also thought to play a crucial role in the disappearance of the Pima paradox (high levels of obesity and diabetes with relatively low rates of cardiovascular disease) (Fagot-Campagna et al. 1999).

Disease Costs and Burden

In the ADA's 1997 measurements, the total cost of diabetes to the nation was approximately $98 billion (ADA 1998). A variety of measures have been used to estimate the economic burden of diabetes in the United States. Most of these include direct health-care costs as well as the indirect costs of lost wages, disability, and/or premature death. The ADA used direct medical costs, such as the costs of blood tests, insulin, and treatment for diabetes-related conditions, as well as indirect costs, including lost productivity. Analyzing these data, the Diabetes Public Health Resource estimated the cost in 1997 to be approximately $12,000/patient; this is four times the estimates for patients in Belgium, Germany, France, and other European countries and the United Kingdom (ADA 1998; IDF 2001; Lieberman 2004).

However, even these gargantuan accounting efforts underestimate the total burden of disease to the country, since a variety of non-health-related factors affect income (e.g., age, gender, education, experience) (Valdmanis et al. 2001). Other studies have tried to elaborate these national statistics with more information on these non-health-related factors. One study simulated a cohort of 10,000 patients, in order to estimate the costs associated with complications of type 2 diabetes (Caroet al. 2002). The researchers came up with a cost of $47,240/patient over thirty years—almost four times the amount estimated by the Diabetes Public Health Resource. Robert Ratner suggests that inclusion of the "intermediate states" of impaired fasting glucose and impaired glucose tolerance, which affect roughly 3 percent of people in the United States, accounts for an additional 12 percent of direct health care costs (Bloomgarden 2003).

Another way of looking at cost is to count the number of deaths attributable to diabetes. Diabetes is not always listed as the cause of death but as a complicating or secondary/tertiary cause on the death certificates and hospital discharge surveys upon which we rely for most of our mortality data (Bertoni et al. 2002). Furthermore, these sources of information do not always give complete information about complicating factors in death or conditions unrelated to the presenting problem at hospital admission. After following 22,044 elders with diabetes for 24 months, Bertoni and his colleagues determined that elders with diabetes have 1.4 times greater mortality in every age group than their counterparts in the general population (Bertoni et al. 2002). That is, elders with diabetes are 1.4 times more likely to die in any given year than their nondiabetic age-mates.

Still other researchers concern themselves with the mental costs and burden of diabetes—the self-perception of daily suffering and disability. Questionnaires that rely on self-report help address some of these concerns, but they are not always used in treatment visits.

The methods for assessing the total economic costs and overall burden of diabetes in the United States continue to change. Direct and indirect costs in 2002 were estimated by the ADA at $132 billion, an increase of $34 billion in five years. Total health expenditures in the United States included in the study totaled $865 billion, of which $160 billion was for people with diabetes (ADA 2003). These costs included $13,243 per patient with diabetes and $2,560 per patient without diabetes. Adjusted for some of the confounding factors mentioned above (e.g., age, sex, ethnicity), people with diabetes spent about 2.4 times more on health care than those without diabetes.

In short, "health care spending in 2002 for people with diabetes is more than double what spending would be without diabetes" (American Diabetes Association 2003:917).

Obesity

Few readers of popular and news media in America are unaware of the most basic condition affecting rates of diabetes in this country: fat. Fat in foods, fat in people, fat in the culture of American foodways.

If any general statement about American diabetes can be made, it is that it is highly associated with obesity (Mokdad et al. 2000; Parker et al. 2001). Diabetes and obesity are the "twin epidemics" (Caprio 2003): the presence of obesity (measured in BMI) correlating highly with the development of diabetes (Knowler et al. 1991; Li et al. 2003).

With rates of obesity rising worldwide at a pace similar to that of diabetes, experts have recently adopted the term "diabesity" to indicate the frequency with which these conditions are encountered together (Zimmet et al. 2001). In the United States, the prevalence of diagnosed diabetes rose from 4.9 percent in 1990 to 6.5 percent in 1998, while the prevalence of obesity increased from 12.0 percent in 1991 to 17.9 percent in 1998 (Mokdad et al. 2001). But there is a substantial delay between the onset of obesity and the subsequent development of diabetes, so the impact that recent rises in obesity rates will have on diabetes rates has yet to be seen.

More than 75 percent of people with diabetes are overweight. That is, the ratio of their weight over height squared (their body mass index, or BMI) is between 25 and 29.9. Higher than that, and the person is classified as obese.[1] According to Lieberman, who wrote an extensive review of the published literature on obesity:

> Overweight and obesity are in excess of 60 percent of the adults among Native Americans (ADA 2002; Hall et al. 1992; Hanley et al. 2000; Joos et al. 1984; Knowler et al. 1990; Young 1996), Mexican Americans (Joos et al. 1984), African Americans (Kuczmarski et al. 1994; Kumanyika 1988, 1993; Lieberman 2000, 2003; Roseman 1985), Native Hawaiian, Samoan, and other Pacific Island populations (Baker et al. 1986; Bindon and Baker 1985; Kumanyika 1993; Zimmet et al. 1995), and populations in

developing countries (Drewnowski and Popkin 1997; Lieberman 2003, 2004: 341; Popkin 1998, 2001).

Data collected by the Indian Health Service's Diabetes Care and Outcome Audit reveal that, among Native Americans, body mass index increased from 32.2 to 33.5 between 1995 and 2001—a shift to extreme obesity levels (Brown et al. 2003). Obesity in African American women is another public health concern, since the prevalence of obesity in this population is twice that of Euro-American women (Flegal et al. 2002). And the prevalence rate of diabetes in African Americans is 1.6 the rate for whites (El-Kebbi et al. 2003).

The body's storage of calories in fat is related to a variety of factors, including food intake, energy expenditure, growth, puberty, fertility, genetics, and insulin sensitivity and secretion (Bloomgarden 2000; VanItallie and Stunkard 1990). Indeed, both obesity and diabetes have been described as a "disease of the brain" for the importance that the hypothalamus—and the hormones it controls—has in their development (Bloomgarden 2000).

Obesity, particularly in the form of adiposital fat (fat that is distributed around the middle of the belly, rather than low around the hips) is the primary risk factor for type 2 diabetes (Joos et al. 1984; Lieberman et al. 1999; Mueller et al. 1984). The adiposital fat distribution pattern often indicates the presence of the insulin resistance syndrome (both fewer insulin receptors as well as insulin resistance). Insulin resistance can precede type 2 diabetes by several years but is also a key factor in cardiovascular disease (Mead 2004). Individuals with comparable amounts of fat stored in the lower body have a much lower risk of illness from hyperinsulinemia, glucose intolerance, and other features of the metabolic syndrome (Montague and O'Rahilly 2000). Higher BMI is associated with female gender, African American and Native American ethnicity, less education, lower income, higher HbA1c, higher fasting blood glucose, and shorter duration with diagnosed diabetes. Controlling for these variables, higher BMI negatively impacted overall quality of life and measures of perceived health, vitality, symptom distress, and psychological well-being (Testa et al. 2003).

So it is important to treat diabetes, in part, through weight loss. Even a small improvement in fitness can improve insulin sensitivity (Bloomgarden 2003). A weight loss of 10 percent of body weight will produce:

- a decrease of 30–40 percent of diabetes-related deaths
- a decrease of 30–50 percent in fasting glucose levels
- a decrease of 15 percent in glycosylated hemoglobin (HbA1c) levels
- a decrease of 15 percent in low-density lipoprotein cholesterol levels
- a decrease of 30 percent in triglyceride levels and
- an increase of 8 percent in high-density lipoprotein cholesterol levels (Mead 2004)

But treatment of obesity can be as laden with cultural mazework as is the treatment of diabetes. David Kozak argues that body image and aesthetic ideals are not only culturally influenced, but enmeshed with perceptions of health and illness. In work among a sample of Pima Indians, the majority of whom were obese, being overweight was not viewed as pathological (Kozak 2005). Further, obese participants tended to view themselves as lighter than they were, as essentially healthy, and as happy with their current appearance. The implications of this research for weight-loss planning in Pimas are profound. And similar cultural or individual assessments of body mass image would be worthwhile for all patients.

Food Abundance

Complicated, like diabetes, by genetic, political-economic, and cultural factors, the obesity problem in America is certainly attributable in large part to the relative food abundance we enjoy: Abundance of low-nutritional-quality but high-calorie, commercial "junk" foods. Abundance of the cheap, high-fat, "fast" foods that play such a crucial role in the economic and cultural pace of our society. And abundance of prepared and preserved meals that not only distance consumers from the original/natural state of foods but also from the process of preparing diverse, healthful meals. This abundance reveals the food priorities of our society: commercial value, speed, and uniformity.

As Hill and Peters report, "Our current environment is characterized by an essentially unlimited supply of convenient, relatively inexpensive, highly palatable, energy-dense foods, coupled with a lifestyle requiring only low levels of physical activity for subsistence." Media pressures aimed at young Americans stress watching television and playing video games while consuming junk food, soft drinks, and eventually beer and cigarettes. A sedentary lifestyle and poor dietary choices are increasingly tied to obesity, which can lead to diabetes in those genetically inclined. Grocery and convenience stores have aisles lined with foods high in fat, calories, and taste, and low in nutrition. Children no longer clamor for their first bicycle as much as they want their first Nintendo. A physician's message of "lose weight and exercise more" can barely be heard over the conflicting messages from television, print advertisements, movies, schools, and peers. (Elder and Muench 2000)

How did we get into this predicament? Well, the explanation might start with the advent of agriculture, which dramatically increased food supplies to human populations. Sometime after about 12,000 BC, the climate in the Near East warmed, allowing plants that could grow, mature, and seed themselves between winters to thrive. But, as archaeologist J. R. Harlan has shown in experiments that recreate the Neolithic agricultural process, ears of wild grain shatter as soon as they reach maturity, dispersing their seeds into the soil for protection (Tannahill 1988). To take advantage of these wild grains, people therefore had to be in the right place at the right time. They settled in camps and, over time, into villages. With the greater availability of grain, domesticated animals could be fed, and the entire dietary balance to which humans had evolved changed (Bloomgarden 2003).

As technological improvements in the agricultural industry have occurred, the amount of energy necessary to harvest grains has been reduced. At the same time, the expansion of markets and people around the globe have increased the diversity of foods available to, at least, the wealthiest in the world, including us in the United States. Indeed, most developed nations enjoy not only a reliable food supply but a diversity of nonnutritious food items like sugar, tea, coffee, and chocolate. This combination of factors has produced the greatest potential for gluttony and obesity in human history.

Two aspects of modern society have created an imbalance between energy intake and expenditure. We have a much more sedentary lifestyle, attributable in part to the adoption of the automobile as the almost singular mode of transportation for the average person in America, making possible city planning and development based on suburbs, extensive highways, and centralized shops and services.

Physical education in high schools decreased from two days to one day per week (Bloomgarden 2003). Related to this, economist Roland Sturm of the RAND Corporation characterized the "lack of safe neighborhoods to walk or bicycle" in as a "market failure" (in Bloomgarden 2003).

The second aspect is the drastic change to the average American meal. Between 1970 and 1990, the typical snack and drink increased in kilocalories from 290 to 450 (Bloomgarden 2003). Fast-food chains have exploded in popularity since their introduction and now offer extra-large sizes. These dietary changes have had a particularly large impact on children's diets: fast foods have increased from 2 to 15 percent of calories in children's diets since the 1970s (Bloomgarden 2003). Brand names for soft drinks and other "junk" foods have been emblazoned on toys, games, movies, education tools, and even baby bottles (Nestle 2002).

The Philadelphia model of prevention, in which city "officials patrol the streets with weighing machines in an effort to persuade locals to lose weight" (Zimmet et al. 2001:786) is a bold, if Hollywood-inspired strategy. Since research has shown that obesity and diabetes aggregate within families, interventions for childhood obesity should target both the child and the overweight parent (Epstein 1996). More long-term solutions will likely require "changes in taxation and reimbursement for health promotion, provision of safe conditions [for exercise] (for example, from assault or traffic) for the elderly and younger sectors of the community, as well as community and workplace access to facilities for exercise" (Zimmet et al. 2001:786).

Complications

As I said in the opening of this book, the complications of diabetes are etched into the memories of Pima Indians. They are the most visible and burdensome aspect of the disease. To begin with, people with diabetes have a significantly reduced life expectancy. The duration of diabetes, in addition to degree of metabolic control, is the key factor in development of complications and premature death. Thus, people who develop diabetes at a younger age die younger. "Patients diagnosed with type 2 diabetes at the age of 13—the average age of presentation among North American children—would lose an average of 14 years of life" (G. Williams 2001).

Complications of diabetes that occur in the small blood vessels include: eye problems like blindness, cataracts, and glaucoma; nephropathy or renal diseases, which are problems associated with the liver; and neuropathy, any problem of the peripheral nerves. Diabetes is the most common cause of adult blindness in developed countries (Amos et al. 1997). Diabetes makes a person 17 times more likely to develop kidney disease. Diabetic neuropathy affects about 30–40 percent of people with either type 1 or type 2 diabetes. Macrovascular complications include coronary heart disease, cerebrovascular disease or stroke, and peripheral vascular disease. For persons with diabetes, these conditions contribute to:

- two to eight times more cardiovascular mortality than people without diabetes
- about twice the incidence of stroke
- about twice the prevalence of hypertension
- a fifteenfold risk of lower-limb amputation

The relationship between diabetes and cardiovascular disease (CVD) is complex; however, studies confirm an increased risk for infection-related death with cardiovascular disease, but not without it (Bertoni et al. 2001). Diabetes-related conditions account for 19.5 percent of all Pima deaths, which is four times that of whites and two times that of blacks (age-adjusted, in Newman et al. 1993; Sievers et al. 1992).

High blood pressure is another chronic condition that is often comorbid with, and so sometimes confused with, diabetes.

CS-M: In your own words, what do you think diabetes is?
Fay: They can't control their, I don't know, their high blood pressure?

CS-M: What do you think diabetes is?
Nancy: High blood pressure and that's all I know about it.

The melding of high blood pressure with diabetes is a clear example of what is more visible to most Pimas and, perhaps, what is more often talked about in social and family settings. Blood pressure is a frequent problem for persons with type 2 diabetes and is also a problem during pregnancy that can lead to complications during childbirth and C-section deliveries.

Pimas' fears of a slow, painful, and withering death to diabetes are therefore warranted. The knowledge Pimas have about the complications of diabetes, not always accurate in biomedical terms, is extensive. The horror of amputation and the pain suffered by relatives undergoing dialysis were profoundly distressing to all of my informants. These emotions are strong motivations for Pima actions, be they preventive actions or ones of avoidance. Particularly for Laura, who watched the slow debilitation of her father as he weakened, got on dialysis, developed an ulcer and an infection on his foot that led to an amputation, and "never gained the strength to get back." After that, Laura said, he gave up.

Since diabetes itself is visible only through a glucose meter, their visceral awareness of this disease comes from observations of its terrible physical impact on the body's organs. Technically diagnosed as "complications" of diabetes, things such as blindness, nerve and circulatory damage, and the need for dialysis are the outward signs of diabetes. And these signs draw upon the fears and disgust of all Pimas from an early age. Maureen, who has had diabetes for several years, is highly motivated by her fear of amputation, hating to "put things off because . . . something like that can happen."

Though Pimas view complications like amputation as the things that indicate death is near, they speak somewhat metaphysically about death by diabetes. Laura, Caroline, and others explained to me that people grow tired of fighting and "give up," rather than being overtaken by the disease. One grandmother took insulin shots every day for years, until one day, she got a blister on her foot. That blister turned into an infection, worsened, and led to an amputation. That amputation did not halt the gangrenous effect, and another was necessary, in Caroline's words, "and they amputated and amputated until the whole leg was gone." When they were going to amputate the other leg, that's when Caroline's best friend's grandmother just gave up and died.

Patients, thus, have some agency even in death by diabetes complications. Complications are the most visible aspect of diabetes and are the stuff from which communal ideas about the disease are made. Every Pima has a memory of these complications through the experiences of family members. These visibly distressing events—amputation, thrice-weekly dialysis, blindness—figure large in the attitudes of non- and prediabetic Pimas toward undergoing tests. If these complications are viewed as the characteristic manifestation of diabetes, then pregnant women may well be surprised to learn they have any form of it. Likewise, in times of health and feeling good, Pimas may conceptualize diabetes as a remote possibility and act accordingly.

And they are no different from the average American. Diabetes may soon reach epidemic proportions across the nation. We are more and more obese, and the fitness craze is a mainly a luxury of well-off Americans. By most measures, the cost of treating the disease and managing its debilitating complications will itself be crippling. If there is any message of hope in this situation, it is the forewarning offered us by the Pimas themselves. Canaries in the mine, the Pimas have offered themselves—their blood samples, their tissue samples, their time, their privacy—for the benefit of the nation's research efforts. Their decline into epidemic, even endemic, diabetes has sounded the warning bell for the nation and the world.

11

Disease of Development

The importance and impact of Pima-based research data on diabetes extends globally. Pimas are known in medical circles more for their diabetes and obesity than for their agricultural genius and long history of hospitality toward Anglos. Their lives and lifestyle have been scrutinized in radio programs, television, popular and scientific magazines, research and clinical journals, and several books. How could one group attract so much attention, when others around the world also suffer from diabetes? Historical circumstances brought the National Institutes of Diabetes, Digestive and Kidney Disorders to their back door, and this has certainly contributed to their fame. But the combination of genetic, historical, and cultural features that converge in the Pimas' story is simply poetic. A more persuasive and gripping story of a culture's transition into modernity could not have been written in Hollywood. Their battle with this predator, this witch, and the battle scars they have to show for it, are cause for alarm to many around the globe.

> Because type II diabetes has affected greater numbers of people from non-European societies who have adapted or have become acculturated to western culture, diabetes for these people has been described by a number of researchers as the "price" of civilization. . . . The path to civilization that Indian tribes were forced to take was set in motion by a rapid succession of events that accompanied episodes of depopulation and colonization. . . . Today, it is not unusual to find tribal leaders attributing many of the social, economic, and health-related problems confronting native peoples to the rapid cultural changes that have been imposed on them. Included in this perspective is the cycle of poverty that is entwined with the almost total dependency on federal and other

governmental institutions—a powerlessness and dependency that to many has indirectly fostered such problems as alcoholism, suicide, homicide, low self-esteem, and the emergence of "new" health problems such as hypertension, cancer, and diabetes. (Joe and Young 1994:5–6)

It seems dozens if not hundreds of studies have been published on the rates of diabetes among Native Americans and other native populations around the world since the middle of the last century. The involvement of culture change in this global increase in diabetes is no longer questioned, though local circumstances vary, of course. In a compelling commentary published by the *Journal of Public Health Management and Practice,* Leandris Liburd and Frank Vinicor summarize the problem by calling attention, first and foremost, to the social production of diabetes and its relationship to the "changing patterns of subsistence, loss of political and economic autonomy, and the subsequent cultural evolution that accompanies these dramatic changes in a population" (Liburd and Vinicor 2003). In high-prevalence communities like Micronesia and Narue, where type 2 diabetes did not exist 50 years ago, its ties to processes of development cannot be denied.

Although a variety of terms have been applied to the problems suffered by groups undergoing rapid cultural and economic change—diseases of development, New World syndrome diseases, the metabolic syndrome, and Syndrome X—there is a reasonable degree of consistency across disciplines about the referent conditions. The metabolic syndrome is defined in endocrinology literature as a collection of risks that increase a person's likelihood of developing heart disease, stroke, diabetes, and obesity. Obesity and its associated gallbladder disease and diabetes are the postulated components of the New World syndrome (Weiss 1985). The term "diseases of development" is an anthropological term that refers to a variety of conditions attributed, at least in part, to culture change (e.g., Cavalli-Sforza et al. 1996; Guerrant et al. 1996; Hunter 1992; Hunter et al. 1983; Kunstadter 1991; McKeown 1985; Nichter 1987; Stock 1986; Szreter 1997), and I use it to collapse these various medical and endocrinological categories together.

Diseases of development are most common among indigenous and other minority populations in developed countries and among the advantaged members of developing societies. The disproportionate development of new type 2 cases in developing countries is associated with "rapid cultural and social changes, ageing populations, increasing urbanization, dietary changes, reduced physical activity, and other unhealthy lifestyle and behavioural patterns" (Amos 1997). For similar reasons, the pronounced increases in diabetes globally are most apparent in non-European populations, including some Native American and Canadian communities, Pacific and Indian Ocean island populations, groups in India, and Australian Aborigines (Zimmet et al. 2001).

All nonwhites in the United States have a prevalence of type 2 diabetes greater than that of U.S. whites (Carter et al. 1996). Part of this trend is attributable to genetic factors and the aggregation of diabetes in families (Gulli et al. 1992). The intrauterine environment also complicates the picture of family aggregation by proposing an environmental, rather than a genetic, relationship between mother and offspring that connotes diabetes risk.

Many of the characteristics effecting the diabetes epidemic in Pimas are similar to the diabetogenic factors operating in other indigenous communities. Diabetes prevalence is three to seven times higher in Hawaiians than whites, and three to four times higher in Filipinos and Japanese in Hawaii than in whites there (Maskarinec 1997). Rapid acculturation into dominant colonial or capitalist cultures has meant abrupt changes in subsistence strategy and corresponding changes in diet and routines of activity (including leisure and work activities). New markets and new market goods move, slowly or rapidly, into the local context, kicking off a transformation not only in local consumption patterns but in the values and attitudes that drive and sustain those patterns. Even when a benevolent development project—for example, in health, sanitation, or potable water—is implemented, there comes with it a variety of influences of questionable goodwill, including differential access to these new resources and potential challenge to or disruption of local authorities.

Such are the dilemmas of "development." As globalization theorists are quick to point out, there are both positive and negative ramifications to the modern interconnection of all the world's cultures. Positive outcomes include greater access to various healing treatments, technological advances in early diagnosis, and access to a greater diversity of both goods and services. Negatively, there are many aspects of culture change—notably dietary change and changes to activity levels concomitant with subsistence strategy change—that contribute to the development of the metabolic syndrome in non-dominant culture groups. Not addressed in this ethnography is the larger constellation of problems stemming from development, including diseases like alcoholism but also social problems like youth violence, unplanned pregnancy, domestic violence, etc.

But diabetes is a specific negative outgrowth that, while multi-faceted and a product of many overlapping causes, cannot be extracted from its political and economic starting place. As Joe and Young put it, the path upon which many tribes were forced has led them to similar outcomes. The Tohono O'odham experienced culture change similar to that of their neighboring "cousins," the Pima, and have similarly high rates of diabetes (Justice 1994). Ben Kracht outlines a similar transformation for tribes in Oklahoma from nomadic hunting and gathering to a sedentary reservation existence (Kracht 1994). Alaska natives have only recently begun to show a rising prevalence of diabetes, a rise that is occurring now among coastal groups of Indians with whom Euro-American contact has been the longest (Schraer 1994.) So, while there is variation across the region, consistent factors of culture change have had a patterned effect on rising diabetes rates.

The attitudes and beliefs about diabetes specific to a given community are particularly important for health interventions, particularly for treatment but also for prevention. For many Native Americans, it is the treatment—not the disease—that is considered the problem (Garcia-Smith 1994).

As change occurs, communities (and individuals within communities) develop new understandings of these circumstances, of their outcomes—including health-related ones—and of the subsequent treatments and explanations offered for those health outcomes. In essence, they make local sense of the diabetes (Lang 1989). More about what makes sense culturally was said in chapter 5. First and foremost, Native Americans with more traditional (less acculturated) worldviews and lifestyles are more likely to explain diabetes in ways consistent with their own cultural framework—perhaps through object intrusion, witchcraft, or breech of a taboo (Joe and Young 1994). For example, when Indian patients with diabetes seek help from tribal healers or practitioners, they often seek the answer to why they were stricken with diabetes. The in-culture interventions that respond to "why" a misfortune or illness has befallen the patient may call for a series of elaborate ceremonies in some tribes, while in others the intervention may call for the use of specially prepared sacred herbs. A cure, therefore, is not always the prime objective, but the ceremonies often are seen as making amends with the source that brought on the illness in order to prevent or lessen the consequences of the disease and/or to enhance the healing power of the remedies prescribed (Joe and Young 1994:12).

Anthropological Models and Contributions

A large cadre of anthropologists, public health professionals, clinicians, and others have made efforts to understand and document the diversity of ideas and attitudes toward diabetes (e.g., Cohen et al. 1994). But within these works are several different theoretical approaches to illness. The very concept of a category of disease produced or made possible by conditions of development is a neo-Marxist one. Urbanization, for example, a demographic change associated with increasing mechanization and segmentation of the food production process frequently generates nutritional disease because of the rapid change in environment and corresponding diet. Medical anthropologists have built models that measure not only the ultimate effects of these changes, but the intermediate ones like stress (Baer et al. 1997; Singer 1990). We have, for example, conceptualized the amount of culture change experienced by a given person using that individual's socioeconomic characteristics, their degree of consumerism (as in the number of cars owned or papers read per week), and their reported perceptions and narrated accounts of stress and adaptation.

Anthropologists have also taken note of epidemiologic data on health trends of communities at different phases of development. Noteworthy has been evidence that, in high-income countries, non-communicable diseases are associated with lower living standards (Townsend and Davidson 1988), while in low-income countries, conditions like obesity and type 2 diabetes are associated with affluence (Brancati et al. 1996; Sobal and Stunkard 1989). Chronic conditions are, therefore, a reflection of the "luxury" of elites in low-income countries, a benefit to which no one aspires.

Bill Dressler's model of "life-style stress" does just this, linking culture change to feelings and perceptions of "dissonance" that, in turn, impact health and other outcomes (1982, 1985). Dressler pro-

posed that modernization is characterized both by economic differentiation and by changes in individuals' style of life, taken as the degree
of engagement in the overall system of economic differentiation and
measured by individuals' consumption of various material goods. He
coined the term "life-style stress" to refer to discrepancies between
lifestyle and economic resources, thereby focusing on material conditions, rather than psycho-cultural ones. In more than two decades of
work, Dressler has used this model to link the results of culture
change with various health outcomes, such as arterial blood pressure.

But several anthropologists, dissatisfied with these bio-cultural
theories, have given preference to the details of history, economics,
and politics on the health of indigenous peoples (e.g., Baer et al.
1997), or to the lived and narrated experience of illness in development contexts (e.g., Lock 1989; Scheper-Hughes 1989, 1991). These—
the critical and interpretive paradigms in anthropology—argue that
the social and cultural contexts of illness have the greatest importance (e.g., Chin-Hong and McGarvey 1996; Dressler 1987; Elliot
1995; Hanna and Fitzgerald 1993; Janes 1990; Pollock 1988). Adler
(Adler et al. 1994), Pearlin (1982), and Dressler (Dressler and Bindon
2000) have also acknowledged that psychosocial processes and individual and personality differences remain relevant, either despite or
within the cultural consonance model.

Some outstanding medical ethnographies have been written on
the impacts of culture change on, for example, indigenous foodways
(Ferzacca 1991; Hill 1997; Lang 1990; Smith et al. 1994), religious
beliefs and practices (Brown et al. 2000; Schoenberg et al. 1998;
Womack 1995), and social expectations (Bissel et al. 2004; Daniel et
al. 1999; Dunn et al. 1990; Hagey 1984; Hunt, Valenzuela, and Pugh
1998; Kozak 1997; Lawson and Rajaram 1994; Pendry 1998; Reid
1992; Scheder 1988; Schoenberg et al. 1998; Williams 2000; Willoughby et al. 2000). Urbanization, for example, a demographic
change associated with increasing mechanization and segmentation
of the food production process, frequently generates nutritional disease because of the rapid change in environment and corresponding diet.

One of the most interesting and, for me, inspiring pieces of research on diabetes is Jo Scheder's look into diabetes among migrant
farmworkers (1988). She was among the first to offer a combination
of ethnographic and biological data on the relationship between dia-

betes and the stress, loss, and separation associated with migratory travel and work. She conducted interviews with Mexican workers migrating seasonally to and around the United States and measured both their stressors and their adjustment using standardized psychological tools. She also collected blood samples to measure dopamine-beta-hydroxylase (DBH), a chemical involved in the synthesis of the hormone norepinephrine, which in turn suppresses release of insulin by cells in the pancreas. These measures, then, speak to the link between social stress and diabetes. In fact, Scheder's work helped expand discussions of the contributing factors to diabetes to include stress and stress-induced physiological states. In particular, she remarked that "obesity-based (BMI) predictions were correct no more often than the perceived stress-based prediction, implying that perceived stress is equally important etiologically" to diabetes as obesity (Scheder 1988:264).

An Unfair Price

Shawna was one of my latest interviews. I interviewed her in her home, a cinder-block, BIA house like most of the ones I had spent time in. She had one wall full of framed 8 × 10 pictures of family members, mostly chubby babies with jet-black hair. Shawna stroked her cat and we talked about her life: her music, some tense relations with family members, a lost job and a new one, and an on-again-off-again romantic relationship. Shawna now had a regular, full-time job and was fairly knowledgeable about diabetes and the importance of diet and exercise in its prevention and control. She was also an extremely well-spoken woman, clearly enjoying and responding to the GED training she was then completing, particularly in literature and English.

Shawna is very much like many Pima women her age: single, trying to finish a GED, working full-time, and balancing both family and romantic relationships—not entirely different from any American woman in her twenties. What was so striking about Shawna was her insight, despite her youth, into the looming specter of diabetes not just for herself but for all her people. Perhaps it was the context of the discussion—the variety of stressful events in her life I've already listed—that pushed her into a mood of general anxiety and depression. But Shawna became tearful, as did I, while talking about a subject now commonplace to us both:

CS-M: In your own words, what is diabetes?

Shawna: A scourge. Diabetes [pause] it's a sign [pause] that this life that we're living isn't our life. [long pause as Shawna begins to cry] . . . This life ain't natural, and the one we had, the one our ancestors had, was way better I think. [pause] This is just the world, like there are just invasive species that comes in and crowds out what was already there. It happens with animals, too, right now. It's just all those unnatural things that want to take over the living world. It's money mostly. But we have things to pull us through, and that saying, "This is supposed to happen." But it's like, if you're not living the way your body's supposed to be living, then you're going to get sick. But it's hard to live the way your body's supposed to be living. You can do it, you just gotta find another way to do it.

Shawna cries because she has inherited a deadly disease, like cystic fibrosis or sickle cell anemia. I was lucky enough to capture her thoughts at a moment of intense insight and intergenerational awareness—perhaps one of many for her, but not something spoken of very frequently by the nondiabetic Pimas I know. She spoke about diabetes as something very specific and real to her, to her parents, like a rare but unambiguously genetic mutation, the effects of which would haunt her most of her life. Anymore, life just ain't natural.

Shawna is a reminder of the emotion of diabetes, and of our human obligations. It is too easy to approach this disease from population statistics, from the historical and economic conditions that had equally predisposed all Pimas, many indigenous groups, and increasing numbers of developing communities around the world. Yet here, sunken into the ultraplush sofa under a poster of Bob Marley, diabetes had again become personal. This type of social inequality is an outrage in Shawna's life.

Is diabetes an economic and social ill, for which the responsibility lies with society as a whole, for which the causal mechanisms are *not* acceptable if unfortunate accidents of history?

Or is it "just how Pimas are"?

Part V

12

Collective Identity, Loner Disease

Given that the epidemic is rooted in both historic events and pre-historic genetic developments, Pimas have had a long time to identify with this disease. Pima women describe diabetes as not simply an individual disease that individuals must fight to control or prevent, but as a community disease that all Pimas understand and adjust to throughout their lives. All Pimas are familiar with their community's diabetes fame, and from this comes the perception, "It's just how Pimas are."

Mary: Yeah, I think Pimas get diabetes more than other people.

Denise: Seems like mostly Gila River, seems like Gila River's about the only one that has more people that are sick from [diabetes].

Sara: I read it, that Pimas have, you know, have a real high risk . . . more than anybody else. You know . . . so that's what I think . . . it's just how Pimas are.

Pimas have developed this perception not only from the epidemic itself, but also from years of research and publicity about their community's struggle with obesity and diabetes (fig. 12.1). Pimas have shared both the benefits and the labels associated with almost four decades of this research, but Pimas struggle with this reputation. They are arguably the most studied ethnic group in the world, having participated in thirty-six years of intensive NIH clinical trials and other studies focused primarily on diabetes and its complications. Kozak argued that diabetes and its complications have, over a long period of high prevalence in this community, led to "changes in . . . individual and collective reasons to [the] disease" (Kozak 1997:348). I agree with this and have found that the complex etiology of diabetes

Figure 12.1. The unpopular media coverage of the Pima diabetes epidemic, titled "A People in Peril" (source: *The Arizona Republic*).

has encouraged community members to maintain nonbiomedical ideas about its etiology, progression, and management.

Diabetes is also something the community is drawing together to fight against. Through small daily acts of resistance to biomedical assumptions, Pimas resist being "preached to" or moralized to by the biomedical community and society at large (Joe 1994). It is a way that Pimas identify with diabetes, because it has become such a familiar part of themselves and their community. Flowing through many of the interactions and discussions in my nine years at Gila River has been a current of Indian identity and resistance to non-Indian political domination. Politically tinged language lamenting the loss of farming and the virtual death of the Gila River in the lives of Pima Indians is frequent in both official settings and in informal talk with me about diabetes. But I do not consider my informants particularly active or activist about treaty rights and Native American self-determination on a daily basis. It is more a response to the constant attention that diabetes draws, and to the pressures Pimas feel to change their health behaviors. Pimas feel this pressure both individually and communally. Individual's choices blend into a collective response and, in Mary Weismantel's words, "in a society under pressure to change, each small act of living becomes a political act" (1997:33).

David Kozak's time with the Pima led him to believe that this community's reaction to diabetes has been built on years of research and treatment with no flagging of prevalence rates. Women experience individual confusion over prenatal diagnostic testing, which they share in dialogue with family and friends, ultimately contributing to a community-wide perception that diagnostic tests are often wrong, or that a positive test one day might be negative next time. Risk information is interpreted in the same way, because plenty of "high-risk" Pimas (less than half of them) never get diabetes. Comorbid conditions also exist for many adults with diabetes, further blurring Pimas' view of diabetes as a distinct disease. Thus, while providers and researchers are increasingly convinced of the high-risk status of all Pima Indians and the importance of weight loss and healthy eating habits, Pimas are becoming increasingly disillusioned by biomedicine's inability to clearly diagnose and halt the epidemic.

Postdevelopment disillusionment with biomedicine is also a theme in Harriet Birungi's work in Uganda (Birungi 1998). There, massive anti-AIDS education campaigns have warned people against the dangers of sharing needles. Injection therapy is one of the most popular forms of therapeutic administration, based in part on its historical attachment to the medical profession. It is trusted as the most effective and safe therapeutic practice. However, Birungi describes a "'sag' in the development process of modern health care" in Uganda where there once was an excellent, respected system of medical experts that held a monopoly over the technology of biomedical care, including syringes. When this monopoly was in place, there was little reason to doubt the effectiveness of its care and its methods. But over time, community members have been able to appropriate expert knowledge to the extent that some laypersons are considered experts in treating certain local diseases. "Consequently, injection giving is now seen as a technical [rather than a professional] exercise" (Birungi 1998:1458).

That this case study involves syringes, an essential tool in the home medical kit of many Pima diabetics, accentuates the irony of Birungi's arguments for the Gila River community. As Ugandan community members gained more information about the AIDS epidemic, they also learned more about the "limits of expertise" and came to demand reassurance in the quality and efficacy of both professionals and their instruments (Birungi 1998:1460). Likewise, as Pimas have learned more about the risks and consequences of diabetes in recent decades, the community has reached a level of understanding that has produced some suspicion about biomedical expertise. Not for the sterility of syringes but for the usefulness of diabetes testing, medication, monitoring appointments, and risk information, many Pimas carry a degree of cynical mistrust (e.g., Barefoot et al. 1998). Theirs is part of a recent skeptical trend "about the validity of biomedical information because of the speed with which biomedical advice to pregnant women has changed" (Browner and Press 1997: 142).

If pregnant Pima women have gained self-confidence in self-care, it relates, I believe, to the community's long experience with diabetes as well as to biomedicine's lack of a cure. When women's trust and confidence in biomedicine—and biomedical providers—wane, their willingness to make some diagnostic and medication decisions for themselves increases. Their self-confidence reflects a refusal to surrender behavioral autonomy or diagnostic creativity to this disease or biomedical institutions. That is, many Pimas agree that no matter what a person does or eats, "if they're going to get diabetes, they're going to get it." Diagnostic criteria for this disease, particularly GDM, remain somewhat open for interpretation.

Women's self-confidence is also supported by a cultural value in the collective, especially on matters related to Pimas' experience of diabetes. This is not to say that women are not independent actors, but that women sometimes speak from a group perspective; that of their female relatives and friends and their collective experiences. They do this through reference to and stories about other women that support their points. Also, because of its epidemic proportion, diabetes can quite literally be seen as a community issue, not an individual one, and therefore not entirely treatable at the level of the individual. A collective response is therefore an appropriate if not a natural one to a collective problem.

That half of all adult Pimas have diabetes seems justification enough for the extensive use of risk data in prevention messages at Gila River. But epidemiological data about groups of people at risk are suited for population-based concerns rather than localized ones (Hayes 1991). Gifford argues that a risk focus in health messages "creates dependent, docile bodies, divert[ing] attention away from structural changes and instead focuses on changing those deemed to be in need" (1986:13). One such risk message is that pregnancy and diabetes are antagonistic states creating lifelong vulnerability for mother and child. This idea has been problematic, largely due to its negative and risk-laden approach to an important and joyful life event. But does it produce docility, dependence, and surrender?

Pressures to reduce rates of diabetes come in the forms of encouragement, funding, education, motivational classes, incentive programs, and research. Refusal to participate in these activities defies pressures to change no matter how well intentioned and is a subtle resistance to domination by biomedical ideologies. But this refusal is a local and even person-specific activity, the occurrence of which is only marginally a resistance "movement" of the kind Scott (1985) describes. Pimas fight biomedical hegemony with the "ordinary weapons of relatively powerless groups: foot dragging, dissimulation, ... false compliance, pilfering, feigned ignorance ... and so on" (1985:xvi).

These are behaviors of Pimas who attend some biomedical appointments but follow instructions and advice selectively, do not share complete health details, and use medications differently than prescribed, as I have described. The ideological pressures of biomedicine take on a moral character, outlining what it is to be a good mother and a good patient. In so doing, new subjective experiences are valued over older, traditional ones. Patients fulfill their sick role with a new awareness of their bodies, informed by technology rather than experience of symptoms. In some ways, diabetes is a thing by which moral worth can be judged. In the biomedical perspective, diseases that can be managed by the patient should be managed by the patient, and patients who do not follow diet and exercise guidelines are considered "noncompliant" and morally wrong for contributing to the disease process.

An element of morality surrounds pregnant women as they try to strike a balance between diabetes prevention and some of the traditional aspects of Pima life. As nearly every provider described them, the Pima have a "strong sense of family and community." But changes related to diabetes prevention and management—such as diet changes, exercise, medication, and monitoring daily glucose—are changes that a diabetic has to do *alone*. Families and friends do not typically help or change along with the patient. Diabetes, the disease that isolates or differentiates a person, is therefore not talked about in a culture that valorizes sociability and togetherness as the Pima do. This is not to say that families are not sympathetic; they are. Families show concern and support by providing rides and company at appointments, child care, and most often a nonjudgmental, "live and let live" attitude toward their behaviors and choices.

But there is also a strong "personal modesty" which prevents Pimas from sharing this disease experience with others, as Joe (Joe 1994) found in a sample of American Indian youths from Apache, Yaqui, Navajo, and Pima reservations. "The process of diagnosis and treatment for most persons with diabetes occurs behind the walls of the clinical building in a one-to-one interaction with a physician or a health worker. . . . 'I do not hide it,' [one grandmother] said, 'but I do not want people watching me stick myself with a needle'" (ibid.: 352). Partnered with the nonconfrontational, "live and let live" cultural value is a confidence that things would work out. Too many times to count, I observed or heard of personal and family crises that required significant economic, time, and social resources to correct. Women's cars broke down in the weeks or days before their due dates; drunken partners and husbands ran off with all of the family's cash, or drank it; electricity or the phone service was cut off. And in each of these scenarios, there was rarely any panic or scurrying to ameliorative action. Reliably, Pimas responded with calm and a sense that everything would be fine—not because funds or help were immediately available, because many women lived without cash, cars, and phone service for months at a time. Instead, Pimas simply did not seem to have the materialism and reliance on these modern conveniences that I had expected. This characterization might seem contradicted by the fact that some Pimas acquire material items (or spend money on gambling or alcohol) with great dexterity and speed. But Pimas do not change their lives in the pursuit of those goods.

To some, the very activities that help prevent or manage diabetes are seen to be colluding with dominant powers. There is some sense that certain behaviors related to good diabetes prevention and management are "white wanna-be" or not traditional.

> **Kelly:** If I don't like the guy or disagree, I'm going to say something. That's the only way to get through it, you know? You got to open your mouth. If you don't open your mouth, then, hey, they're just going to walk all over you. So, you know, it's one way or the other . . . some people would say I'm acting "white," saying something . . .
>
> **CS-M:** And people call that "white"?
>
> **Kelly:** Yeah, like you think you know too much, or you're too good, or whatever.

Acting "white" includes using big words (reflecting a medical knowledge about diabetes), not eating traditional foods or preferring diet foods, exercising (especially nontraditional forms of exercise like aerobics and weight lifting). Equating certain health-oriented behaviors with "white wanna-be" attitudes reveals a powerful traditionalist stimulus impacting women during pregnancy and throughout life. Kunitz has argued that seeking health care for prevention purposes is a behavior that indicates a high degree of incorporation into biomedical ideologies of health (Kunitz 1983:3–4). Bolstering this are ideas about the dangers of seeking medical care, including providers' ability to sap your personal strength and esteem, and the likelihood of conjuring up diabetes through too much talk about it.

Women's talk about elders, and the accounts of a few elder women, reveal some symbolic ties between elders, tradition, and antibiomedical sentiment. Of all age groups, elders are most likely to avoid or reject care, for the same reasons that we have already discussed for pregnant women.

CS-M: Why do you think some Pimas don't like going to the doctor?

Laura: I think a lot has to do with their philosophy, depends on how old they are. Some of them believe in just strictly Indian medicine, and some people probably are in denial and don't go unless they really have to . . . and then just people's own experience. If they had a good experience, bad experience, and you repeat—and, you know, [it] happens in your family. And it's just a domino effect. So it depends where they're coming from.

But elders are also seen as closer to or more likely to receive a diagnosis of diabetes. Their health-care-seeking practices are more often tied to concerns about this disease or others. And fear is generally assumed to motivate their avoidance of care.

Ethel: I don't know. I just get scared sometimes.

Vina: I think mainly because [my dad] is scared . . . probably about what they say. But usually he doesn't really go, and there's a lot that don't want to go. . . .

Catherine: They're scared. There's one lady I knew she had a big old sore on her leg. She was a diabetic. She was scared that they were gonna have to amputate her leg.

Elders were also thought to be more likely to prefer traditional remedies to biomedicine.

Denise: I think some of the older people are scared. . . . I don't know, they have their own beliefs and stuff like that there's a lot of them that's why they don't go see the doctor because they feel that medicine won't really work for them. They'd just rather do it their own way or the old way whatever.

Rosalie: Because they don't want to get help for themselves. They're scared, some are scared. Some don't want help. Some just want to do their own thing.

Fear, specifically, of being diagnosed with diabetes can become the greatest motivator against going in for care.

Dorothy: They know that they're gonna be diabetic, and they see what the older people [went through] when they had gotten sick and stuff. You know, it's probably scary for them, and they don't want to go through that. . . . Some people say, "Well, we didn't need that a long time ago," and that's their way of dealing with it. It's just like that, and so it's the hardheaded ones.

Elders and others believed that the diagnostic process was a specific danger to be avoided. Indeed, behind their reported reasons for avoiding care seemed to be the belief that speaking to biomedical providers about a diagnosis of diabetes, and allowing diagnostic efforts to be made, might make one more sick—perhaps even bring on diabetes.

Fay: Yeah I think . . . a long time ago when they had traditions, I think, you know, they believed that their medicine, they didn't get sick as much as they do now, now that they have doctors. I think most of the people got . . . because I guess they're afraid of what's gonna happen or what they're gonna say or are they gonna get sick more . . . they think, you know, like I remember my mom. Before she died she never went to the hospital, she wasn't gonna go. And we always told her to go because she had breathing problems, and that's how she died. It's like to her it was like if you go to the doctor, you know, you get sick more. Because I guess you'd find out what's wrong, and they try to treat it and all that. To her it was like she didn't want to do that. She didn't want to go to the hospital, and she didn't want to have to do none of that.

Other Americans hold beliefs related to the "awakening" or "activation" of disease through physician intervention or probing (Hoffman-Goetz and Mills 1998; Kavanagh and Broom 1998:440). The feeling that going to the hospital would begin the slippery slope of diagnosis and declining health is a "subjective probability" that Pimas manage by refusing to begin the process (Gifford 1986). In this way, Pimas can be seen to be preventing diabetes with prophylactic avoidance. When risk information is unclear, the boundary between a healthy-but-at-risk state and the diseased state becomes blurred. In the case of diabetes, the predisease or "high-risk" state might be easily transformed into "outright" diabetes by the careless verbal conjuring of providers. This avoidance behavior has been questioned both among the Pima (Kozak 1997) and in other communities (e.g., Lewis 1993), because it appears, at first, to be denial.

Whether "surrender," "learned tolerance," fear of "awakening," or just plain denial, Pimas do reject biomedical care even when they are in pain, are fearful about their health, or have symptoms that impede their regular activities. These are preventive behaviors—preventive of at least one form of harm that the care itself would produce. Further, these preventive, prophylactic attitudes and behaviors can be directly linked to the mysterious and confusing nature of diabetes and risk.

Death is widely recognized as a topic that is considered taboo by many tribes. "To speak at length about death is often believed to predict the death of the person being spoken about" (Reid and Rhoades 2000:422). Similarly, diabetes—probably because of its close association with death and illness—receives the same taboo associations at Gila River, where the diabetes epidemic claims the lives of more every year. At risk in openly examining oneself for diabetes is not only one's reputation among family and social supports for genuine community membership or allegiance, but also one's very health. For Pimas, "health" cannot be boiled down into a number (i.e., a glucose reading) but is instead a question of personal strength and viability. It is increasingly recognized as, perhaps, a pan-Indian quality that one must avoid the confrontational gaze or risk becoming confrontational oneself. Health-care interactions that conjure disease or court risk by speaking too much or too directly about diabetes are inherently harmful to the individual. The clinical encounter affects one's personal strength and viability, which is directly linked to one's ability to ward off diabetes.

13

Pregnancy Stories

The old tribal offices sit in the middle of Sacaton, just about a block off one of the main roads through the reservation. The single-story brick building is not labeled well and was hard to find, since the streets aren't labeled either. But my visits there became so frequent that I soon learned not only its different entrances but when I could get away with parking in the favored, unmarked spot under the one scrubby tree that provided any shade.

During the months when I was so frequently at the tribal offices gaining necessary permissions to begin formal interviews, I had made friends with a few of the tribal secretaries. These women took the meeting minutes, managed all the paperwork and several of the appointments for tribal committees, and generally kept the business of government rolling along for a nation of more than 12,000 members. Their tenure in these positions could last for many years, though tribal council members would come and go. That longevity, no doubt, was key to their success. Although the business of the tribal council is serious and members' attitudes normally stoic, the council secretaries are warm and inviting. I still see them whenever I get the chance.

On one particular morning, I was talking casually with one of the secretaries about her family and her health. She'd heard of me from the other secretaries and had plans to give me a formal interview later. But her niece, she said, lived just across the street. And she thought her niece was pregnant! I jumped at any opportunity to meet pregnant women. "Tricia might do your interview. You should just walk over and ask her."

Walking out the back door of the tribal offices and toward the blue house that had been described to me, I quickly saw the telltale signs of a young family: scooters and deflated balls, all faded by a life outside, punctured by the many cacti around. Without an escort or invitation, I knew my arrival, especially on foot, would be taken as strange and perhaps threatening. No one answered my knock, and I knew that might well be the discerning action of someone peeking from behind a curtain. As it turned out, I had knocked on the wrong door anyway. Tricia's house was 50 yards away. When I finally figured that out, Tricia answered the door and was as friendly, although somewhat shy, as her aunt had been.

Tricia has a patient, gentle face. She listened to my introduction as her children—several of them with their heads popping out from behind her—watched their mother welcome this strange Milga:n (Anglo) into their home. I explained the project, the interviews, the payments, the topics. All the while, she nodded in assent and said she understood the project and was willing to participate. Not until 10 minutes later did Tricia finally say, "We've met before. I talked to you at the prenatal clinic."

She then let slip the kindest but most sincere giggle I've ever heard, both teasing and consoling. It released me to blurt out an embarrassed guffaw. And so began—a second time—my close friendship with Tricia.

Tricia laughs more easily and frequently than anyone I've ever known. Laughter would be the foundation of our relationship. She signed on not only for the project interviews but invited me for visits and socializing, and called on me for favors and errands (which were, of course, not only a pleasure but of great interest to me as an anthropologist). She confided in me about her hopes for her family, her career goals, her marriage and extended family—far beyond the topics of the formal interviews. Our due dates were within a few weeks of each other, and she was free with advice and conversation about pregnancy.

Despite being several years younger than me, Tricia had four other children. She did not have diabetes, has been unemployed most of the time I've known her, and was generally positive about her health care. Like many Pima women at her stage in the life cycle, she stayed at home with kids while her partner was supposed to be working or looking for work. Tricia's longtime partner (the father of all Tricia's children) made good money when there was a contract job he could fill. Inside, a large table with benches on either side separated the large kitchen area from the family room. The latter was buried under a landslide of children's toys and books and an occasional magazine. This was a playroom, mostly, and the happy children of this family used it until its seams burst, its walls cracked, and its flooring disintegrated. Everything in the house was well used with love—a full breakfast table, when I arrived unreasonably early; sofas brimming with jiggling, crawling bodies; army-size cooking pots and dishes faded from millions of scalding hot washes.

Tricia and her partner had a broken-down car in the yard that he could occasionally, miraculously fix. Their home was also typical: given over largely to the children. The yard was large and essentially unaltered desert except for the ramada built onto the front of the house using mismatched pieces of plywood, and their assortment of dogs and cats.

Tricia was thrilled to be pregnant, as she had been every time before. She enjoyed and rarely missed her prenatal appointments. She loved her doctor, and although she said she would probably never express any disagreement with her, Tricia also admitted that she never *had* any disagreements. She followed instructions, tried to eat well, and got a good deal of exercise running after, cooking for, and cleaning up after her family. She even borrowed a book on pregnancy from her field nurse,[1] and she talked with me often about what it said.

Mary was a less regular informant and companion because of her remoteness. There are parts of the reservation that are so off-the-beaten-trail that they harbor palpable memories of nineteenth-century Pimeria. Mary's home is in one such place. A baby blue mobile home is now part of the compound. Situated under a lone tree, this site is just a hundred yards or so away from what had been the alluvial plain of the Gila River. The family sandwich house still stands and is abutted by a large and welcoming ramada. In all, this homesite accommodates the family—Mary and her boyfriend, their first child, Mary's brother, and Mary's parents—with room to spare.

Finding the place was an exercise in faith: faith in my improving but still nascent ability to extract coherent directions from my informants. This journey was a greater test than most, since it would traverse a couple of miles of dirt road, rather than the unmarked paved roads of Sacaton, and lay alongside an interstate highway, heightening my sensitivity to the intrusiveness of that modern convenience in what was otherwise isolated, silent desert.

Mary was one of those favorite but frustrating women who enjoyed but missed several of her prenatal appointments because she had no transportation. Mary was 18 when I met her, in her second trimester of pregnancy, and already had a nine-month-old baby. She also had gestational diabetes. Mary liked her doctor and the prenatal appointments very much, particularly because she enjoyed talking with providers about her pregnancy and her other son. She was particularly fond of Joan, the nurse whom I discussed in chapter 7, and her doctor. I gave her a ride once but, like the clinic staff, had a terrible time reaching Mary by phone. A couple of unannounced trips out to her house were also fruitless. She and the others were gone, and the compound was as still as the breezeless, hot air. But Mary remained a favorite acquaintance, for her enthusiasm about pregnancy and her children, if not for glucose control.

Field Notes—1/5/00, Prenatal Appointment with Stephanie

When I arrived at her house, Stephanie[2] [age 22] was yelling at Sarah to find her other shoe. I've never known her to yell but when I saw her I could tell it was because she was nauseous with "morning sickness." This was her third pregnancy. Her mom was diabetic but Stephanie said she wasn't "yet." She knows she's "borderline," though, because "during my pregnancy with Toby, they told me I was—but then after he was born, they changed their minds." She interpreted this as meaning she was "'borderline' diabetic."

Stephanie had only gone to one appointment in this pregnancy—she's now 31 weeks gestation. She told me she'd attend today because she knew they would do an ultrasound, and wanted me to give her a ride the four blocks to the hospital. She also wanted to ask to switch hospitals. [No labor and delivery dept. at the reservation hospital.] At Central Hospital, she said, they were "rude" and treated you like they didn't care." "And they're even Indians!," she said [Central is an IHS hospital]—"but they're 'city Indians' and think they're all better."

She had a burrito for breakfast [2 eggs, 1 cup potatoes, ¼ cup onions, ½ cup beef, 18″ tortilla]. Her appointment was for 8:30. We arrived at 8:00 and sat with a friend. She had a Coke while she waited, and was called at 8:30 to update her record and give a urine sample. At 9:00 she was called back by the nurse for vitals and "all the questions."

When she spoke to the nurse, she was reminded that she was supposed to have fasted, but Stephanie didn't admit to having had breakfast. She had blood drawn later that morning at the lab and would have to return in a couple of days for results. [This was for diabetes screening, but Stephanie didn't remember that.]

At home she talked about how getting back to the hospital this month would be a "pain" because it was winter and too cold to walk. Her mom had been getting sick a lot lately and wasn't able to watch the kids, so she'd have to take them with her. And "whenever you did take your kids, the staff looked at you real 'snotty' if they would make any noise or touch anything. And, of course, Sarah was into everything." And they would always give her a lecture about how Toby was too chunky, and "you shouldn't be letting him drink that." These were the main reasons she didn't go to prenatal appointments. "They usually only have you pee in a cup and listen to the baby's heartbeat. So if I feel fine, there wasn't much reason to go—except for that ultrasound picture."

Field Notes—1/12/00,
Prenatal Follow-Up with Stephanie

Stephanie told me she wasn't going to go, but her mom had an appointment with podiatry the same day, so we all went together. Stephanie talked to the nurse, who said her sugars were high and she had to talk to the people over at Diabetes Education. Toby drew a couple of glares, I noticed, from a secretary for spilling his Coke on the floor. At Diabetes Education, they were telling her she was diabetic—230 sugars—and that it was going to hurt the baby if she didn't get it under control. Stephanie later told me, "the only reason it was so high is because of that breakfast burro, so I'm probably still just 'borderline.'"

[Stephanie missed the education class scheduled for her at Diabetes Education at the end of October. Had baby boy 11/—/00, cesarean, 10# 10z. He had jaundice and a very slight heart murmur.]

14

Conclusion
Facing a Predator

It's a fearsome predator. To fight it requires an individual's lifelong commitment to dietary change, exercise, and self-monitoring—if not also a medication regime (oral or injectable) and perhaps even dialysis. It also requires the work of a team of health providers—internal medicine or family practitioner, diabetes educator, nutritionist, podiatrist, dentist—ideally in regular communication with one another. This entire group must move as a unit whenever the patient's health changes. To control diabetes thus demands a gargantuan effort in the lives of individual sufferers and their providers.

To actually reduce diabetes rates across an entire community or nation demands nothing short of revolution.

Anthropologists are not social engineers, and it would be unprofessional and perhaps unethical of me to prescribe a course of action out of the Pima epidemic, even if I could. I would also risk losing friends, as Tohono O'odham Suzan Shown Harjo learned when she published her New Year's resolution to reduce the amount of fry bread in her diet and encouraged others to do likewise (Harjo 2005). So many core cultural values are involved in diabetes (e.g., motherhood, foodways, ethnic identity) that Pimas could not help but feel threatened on political and symbolic levels. Pimas take serious offense at the unbidden advice of outsiders.

But what will happen if the average age at diagnosis drops to around 20 years, making many Pima pregnancies diabetic at conception? The implications for congenital anomalies are profound, and the likelihood of pandemic quite high. If the high cost and limited availability of healthy foods already make prevention difficult for adults, pregnant teens will be doubly challenged. Alternatively, the prenatal period could signal our best hope of curbing this epidemic. The average age of diabetes diagnosis *could* be raised.

Diabetes rates can be reduced at Gila River. And I don't think it will be a result of better, faster medical care. It will neither be something that individual patients produce. Instead, it will be the result of a community transformation—a change to some pervasive elements of society that support the status quo.

Many before me have pointed to the importance of culture in this and other groups' (e.g., Mexican American) diabetes rates, and I don't argue with these statements. Indeed, I have made them myself in this book. But these cultural elements do not have a lock on Pimas. Culture is as adaptive as it is maladaptive. The Pima "culture" has at various times taken on commodity foods, wage labor, Christianity, and enlistment in the U.S. military, when circumstances made these changes necessary or beneficial. Culture will likewise change when some individuals won't or can't. So the "culture as barrier" to diabetes prevention is an erroneous application of anthropological knowledge. Indeed, it is a position that blames the victim by attributing to them a social and attitudinal disability. In reality, it is culture and the processes made possible by communal attitudes, shared activities and ideas, and common history that will launch the Pima out of this epidemic.

To recognize the power of circumstances (particularly disease epidemics) to motivate change, we need only consider U.S. history. In the late 1800s, when cholera, diphtheria, and tuberculosis epidemics raged in most urban metropolises around the world, the U.S. Public Health Service established itself as a credible and capable authority. Through leaders like Drs. Charles Hewitt, T. Mitchell Prudden, and Hermann Biggs, the Public Health Service was given the political and economic resources it needed to enforce policies that would control and prevent the spread of infectious disease (Garrett 2001). There was a "culture," if you will, of intolerance for disease, and that state was mandated by society to take control of the situation. Their response included aggressive sanitation campaigns, quarantines of the ill, and mandatory (and if necessary, forced) immunizations.

Few today would advocate such a strong-arm approach to the public's diabetic health.[1] Citizens would not likely tolerate it. But if diabetes were viewed as transmissible from mother to fetus in utero, we almost certainly would see greater surveillance and treatment of pregnant women to guarantee prenatal glucose control.[2]

Public health policy is not a question of whether individual rights can be abridged—because they certainly have been in cases where the threat to a fetus or to the greater public has been established. It is a question of when—when communities will decide that the threat of an epidemic warrants stronger measures. In this sense, each community determines its own tolerance for disease. In the late eighteenth century, a critical mass of Americans living in crowded cities was willing to tolerate certain restrictions and duties. The unwilling remainder was, like Typhoid Mary, too small or too weak to stop them.

Neither Pimas nor Americans may decide to strong-arm citizens into losing weight or giving up fry bread. Instead, we place hope in the possibility that less oppressive forms of persuasion will convince a critical mass to change voluntarily. And this critical mass will then help transform the entire community.

At Gila River, this critical mass will include types like Shawna, whose sense of injustice over this disease is so great, and like Mary, Ethel, and Violet, whose sense of motherhood includes certain differences in how they talk to their children about health and disease. It will also involve the leadership of elders, who retain great prominence in the community, and tribal healers, who typically now train under a Tohono O'odham but who seem to be increasingly known about and called upon at Gila River. Doctors and diabetes educators will also have a role, especially those who are willing and understand how to transition power out of the hospital and into more community-based action.

Diabetes is a civic injustice that must become a rallying point for Pimas. Too much now rests on providers' ability to encourage Pimas' enrollment in, completion of, and behavioral responses to diabetes education. It is cultural factors that are most often targeted in clinical and public health interventions: dietary habits, values about exercise, orientation toward the body and self-monitoring, ideas about individual responsibility for health, and even attitudes toward health care. Even "public health" interventions are aimed at individuals, while larger structural and institutional barriers are left unaddressed.

But the very hospital in which these interventions occur—while providing excellent acute care, centralized services, and standardized treatment—may not be a good model for communities in which the population is dispersed, mobility is reduced, and cultural differences in the doctor-patient relationship are great. In those settings, decentralized or satellite clinics and home nursing services would better serve the needs of remote residents on the reservation. These forms of care require different support structures (e.g., supervision and management of multiple "roaming" providers with portable offices, travel funds, and mobile equipment). Existing community structures should be exploited, with education and care occurring in community centers, fitness centers, and homes.

Structural change must also reach beyond the clinic and its services. If the NIDDKD were able to adopt a more proactive, community-based (rather than research-bound) approach to diabetes prevention, it might allocate a portion of its $1.6 billion annual budget to structural changes on the Gila River Indian Reservation, such as:

- The recruitment of more employers of high school graduates (and GED holders) to the reservation
- The growing and/or marketing of an affordable variety of fresh produce, made accessible to all members of the community
- The planning and construction (or redesigning) of neighborhoods to promote safe, outdoor, nonmotorized travel and recreation
- The hiring of more teachers for reservation jobs, at higher pay, including ones who specialize in behavior management and at-risk children. And truancy officers need more resources to effectively do their job.

The world owes a huge debt of thanks to the Pimas for the knowledge of diabetes they made possible. More than receiving thanks, I think, they would like to be viewed for their resilience, their adaptability, and the strength of cultural and family ties uniting them against this common predator. Most tribal leader friends of mine chafe under the tribe's reputation for diabetes and obesity. Certainly, they share many commonalities with the 151 million adults worldwide with this disease. Likewise, communities in Asia or Africa could be identified, where the fastest growth in diabetes rates is estimated. So could several in the United States, where (in 1997) we spent $98 billion on our more than 10 million citizens with the disease. Pimas are also not the only Americans that struggle with obesity—almost 20 percent of Americans are obese. This is the principal factor in the increase in diabetes rates.

The Pima transformation out of this epidemic is brewing and will be marked by change in all sectors of Pima life. Much like their experience of the last 150 years, the next 50 will produce both adaptive and maladaptive cultural change. As Pimas become more discerning about medical care in their community, they will make decisions about how to structure and restructure future efforts. They will make changes that produce not bodies free of symptoms, nor pregnancies free of risk, but lives free of diabetes. Their attention will be on healthy and valued lives lived in safe communities, among healthy families, and in energized movement. Prevention is already taking on dimensions completely foreign to the hospital setting, such as in church sermons and parenting classes. As they prepare for the destruction of this *ho'ok*, the most influential Pima will be acting for the benefit of all community members, for all tribal nations, and for the world. Pimas know more about this disease and how to fight it than anyone else. So they will certainly know best how to be rid of it.

Appendix A

Market Price Comparison

Food	Sacaton market price ($)	Coolidge supermarket price ($)
Q. oats (42 oz)	3.49	3.09
J. peanut butter (13 oz)	2.49	2.29
R. enriched white bread (24 oz)	0.99	1.07
Macaroni and cheese (7.25-oz box)	2/0.89	2/0.89
GM all-purpose flour (5 lb)	1.99	1.89
BY vegetable oil (32 oz)	2.29	1.99
Whole milk (gallon)	3.19	2.89
Ground beef	1.69/lb	1.49/lb
Cucumber	0.89/each	0.49/each
Total	18.91	16.09

Note: recorded in winter 2000

Appendix B

Districts and Locations Represented in Ethnographic Interviews

Districts Represented

District 1, Blackwater	1
District 2, Sacaton Flats	2
District 3, Sacaton	28
District 4, Stotonic	4
District 5, Casa Blanca	8
District 6, Gila Crossing	16
District 7, Pee Posh	2
Off-Reservation	2

Location of Interviews

Participant's home	47
Carolyn's home	1
Participant's work	6
Restaurant	3
Service center	6

Appendix C
Summary of Focus Groups

I conducted focus groups primarily to explore the degree of cultural consensus that might be found at Gila River regarding diabetes. Had recruitment efforts for these groups been more successful, I would have used more of these data in my discussion. That the group format was not as successful as individual interviews may itself be important information for health education programs. Three women (all of whom were pregnant) attended focus group #1, and five persons (four women, including one pregnant woman, and one man) attended focus group #2. All nonpregnant women and the man had diabetes, while the pregnant women did not. Each focus group was held at a District Service Center, where most district events take place. After the ubiquitous and obligatory socialization and food, the educational materials on the following page were reviewed and discussed.

Participants were asked to discuss which pamphlets first "caught their eye" and which they were most likely to pick up and read in a doctor's office. I then had them elaborate on the features (e.g., charts, font size, pictures, format of the information) that were most and least useful or comprehensible to them. Unstructured discussion about information received from doctors and how patients spend their time at the doctor's office (e.g., waiting, reading educational materials) was encouraged and, to a moderate degree, obtained.

The pamphlets that were most popular were #2 ("Prenatal Care"), #3 ("Problems During Pregnancy"), #8 ("Type 2 Diabetes in Native Americans"), and #9 ("Diabetes and American Indians"), for several reasons. First, information was laid out in tables or bullet-point format, making it easy to read. One participant remarked about #8 ("Type 2 Diabetes in Native Americans"), "This is something I would keep on my refrigerator." This remark seemed to reflect a common perception that pamphlets and handouts should be direct and concise,

Focus Group Discussion Materials

Pamphlet number	Focus group discussion materials
1	"Breastfeeding Your Baby" by ETR Associates © 1995
2	"Prenatal Care" by ETR Associates © 1995
3	"Problems During Pregnancy" by ETR Associates © 1995
4	"Pregnancy Facts" by ETR Associates © 1995
5	"Planning for Pregnancy When You Have Diabetes" by the Indian Health Service © 1995
6	"Gestational Diabetes: What It Means for Me and My Baby" by the American Academy of Family Physicians
7	"Screening for Diabetes During Pregnancy" in *The Informer*, vol. 4, no. 4, 1998
8	"Type 2 Diabetes in Native Americans" by the Diabetes Education Center © 5/99
9	"Diabetes and American Indians" by the Indian Health Service © 1987
10	Several advertisements from *McCall's* (May 2000) and *Health Magazine* (April 2000)

with clear wording and only moderate amounts of pictures. Pamphlets that gave paragraph-format information were considered "too long" or too full of jargon (particularly #6). Although participants did not voice this analysis, it appeared to me that pamphlets written in "Q & A" style were not particularly effective, because they were too wordy (e.g., #5 and #6).

Second, although pictures were popular, they were not considered essential in a pamphlet that participants "would pick up and read." Instead, the visual clarity of the information was more important, that is, a lack of clutter or too much wording. Pictures were, however, appreciated in pamphlets #1 and #4, since these pictures illustrated the steps of breastfeeding and the stages of labor, respectively.

The third trend identified through the focus groups was a desire for Native American-specific information about diabetes and pregnancy. Pamphlets #3, #8, and #9 addressed information—and addressed it in a format—that was of immediate relevance to the Pima participants. The information in two of these three pamphlets was basic educational information about diabetes, especially its prevalence in Native Americans and the specific challenges that Native Americans face. While many of the pamphlets had general information about diabetes, and most had multicultural figures or photos, the pamphlets specifically tailored to the needs of Native Americans were of great interest. When questioned about this, one woman said, "I've learned about the basics (of diabetes) at the hospital already. This tells me some things I don't know about Indians in particular."

Notes

Chapter 1

1. A governor, lieutenant governor, and 17 council members are elected to rotating terms of three years. The Gila River Indian Community has been acting under a constitution and bylaws since 1934, so it is no surprise that the frequent meetings I attended were all run using *Robert's Rules of Order*. The council divides into five different standing committees to deal with the work of the tribe: Health and Social, the committee that evaluated, approved, and supervised me in my work; Governance and Management; Education; Legal; and Natural Resources.

2. The Hu Hu Kam Memorial Hospital is tribally owned and houses the Diabetes Education Center (DEC). Public health nursing, environmental health services and other Indian Health Service (IHS) programs are active on the reservation. The IHS trains community health representatives, about 21 of whom work on the reservation—most in the public health services. There are also offices for tobacco tax funding; Women, Infant and Children (WIC) services; Head Start; and various tribal services. There is a wellness center gymnasium and weight room in Sacaton. There are also District Service Centers in each district of the reservation, in which bi-monthly community meetings, elders' lunches, elections, memorial services, and local project meetings are held. The service center is the largest structure in most districts and provides the only air-conditioned meeting space in some districts. The service centers are, therefore, where public health clinics (e.g., "Well-Baby Clinics," where immunizations are available) are held and where I held the focus groups for my project.

Chapter 2

1. Between 24 and 160 of these brick houses might exist in what look like developments or tracts. Three such tracts exist in Sacaton, the largest settlement on the reservation and the location of most government offices. There

are two other areas of centralized population—marked by the presence of a gas station and convenience store. The alternatives to tribal housing include *olás ké* (traditional round houses), "sandwich" houses constructed by sand-wiching adobe between wooden 2″ × 8″ slats, and trailer homes. These types of homes are more common outside of the population centers. Only the trailers have both electricity and plumbing.

2. Gila River employment rankings benefit from its two casinos, and in-dustrial parks employ almost 250 Pima workers. A handful of Pima families continue to farm, and the tribe collectively runs a farm of 12,000 acres supporting cotton, wheat, millet, alfalfa, barley, melons, pistachios, olives, citrus, and vegetables. In 1999, the total agricultural product value of the tribal farm was more than $25 million. Very few Pima women work for the tribal farm, although many are employed by the tribal government, hospital, and casinos (U.S. Bureau of the Census 2000).

3. Certification as a diabetes educator requires an advanced degree in a clinical field (e.g., nursing, nutrition, occupational therapy), at least two years of experience in professional practice, at least 1,000 hours of diabetes self-management education experience, and passing a certification examination for diabetes educators.

4. These formal recruitment efforts took place at: Hu Hu Kam Memorial Hospital's Prenatal Clinic; Sacaton W.I.C. Office; Gila Crossing Prenatal Clinic; Gila Crossing W.I.C. Office; and Diabetes Education Classes (all districts of the reservation).

Chapter 3

1. I use the colloquial "outright" diabetes to describe type 2 diabetes in Pima Indians. This is the term they use to distinguish between diabetes that disappears after the birth of the child (GDM) and diabetes that stays on.

2. The first maternal A1c level is of interest in questions of miscarriage or fetal demise. If that first A1c reveals high blood glucose, then this may have created a toxic uterine environment for the fetus in the critical first eight weeks of pregnancy. These types of congenital malformations include heart murmur and neural tube defects. Rates of spontaneous abortions have been shown to correlate with A1c levels during the first trimester. My review of the fourteen cases of fetal demise revealed: five cases had no A1c levels; eight women had A1cs that were out of control ($\geq .06$); and one was in control. High maternal glucose may thus have contributed to fetal health problems in eight cases and possibly in some of the five cases where no maternal glucose was recorded. Fetal demise rates of 8–12 percent of pregnancies in all years but 1998 (which was 20.8 percent) are not abnormal for diabetic populations. Fetal demise/miscarriage rates as high as 30 percent among persons with diabetes have been reported.

Of the sixteen deliveries by cesarean section (28 percent of all births), nine had a congenital malformation or other perinatal morbidity. Seven were in mothers with gestational diabetes; five were in mothers with preexisting diabetes; and one was unidentified by class in the medical record. Risk of congenital malformations among infants of diabetic mothers ranges nation-wide from 6 to 12 percent (Kitzmiller et al. 1978; Reece and Hobbins 1986). The results from this study (14 percent, n = 8) are therefore high. However, this study revealed certain problems in consistent documentation. Recording professionals noted thrush and low birth weight as congenital malforma-tions. Removing these inappropriate and uncertain notations yields an 11 percent congenital malformation rate: a rate within the national range. Other perinatal morbidity (46 percent, n = 26) included high birth weight (19 percent, n = 11), which can be associated with diabetes in the mother.

Chapter 4

1. One study of patient/provider interactions in a diabetes clinic showed that patients and their providers disagree roughly 20 percent of the time on the issues discussed and decisions made during an appointment (Parkin and Skinnert 2003). So communication is not an uncommon problem in diabetes care generally.

Chapter 5

1. Semantic networks are the "diverse meanings, voices, and experiences that are condensed by core symbols in the medical lexicon" (Good 1977; Good and Del Vecchio Good 1994:171). These core symbols allow women to inte-grate diverse and, sometimes, conflicting pieces of information about their experiences.

2. Another view of women's reproductive health comes from the social and cultural analysis of the body. This analytical lens organizes talk about wom-en's health in terms of the phenomenological experience, her body as a stage for interactions in the world, an object into and onto which events have their impact, and the "thing" through which she expresses and feels these experi-ences. Martin's analyses of historical trends in the treatment of women give an especially clear example of this perspective as it is applied to not only patterns in history but also a contemporary case study in women's and men's health.

3. Ninety-eight percent of all births in the United States occur in hospitals.

4. Their research with women undergoing Pap smears to screen for cervi-cal cancer revealed that many women reacted to a cervical abnormality "as if they had no risk previously" (1998:440).

5. The average age of participants was 28.5 years old. The women ranged

in age from 18 to 67, although I spoke to quite a few younger teenagers informally, and to elder family members of some women. Most of the pregnant women were in the twenties or early thirties, although a majority of women had their first child in their teen years. Thirty-four (71 percent) of the participants had children, and 17 (27 percent) reported they had diabetes.

6. All names are pseudonyms.

7. Several things may contribute to a person's sense of vulnerability, including emotional states or culturally determined periods of vulnerability. Likewise, people will have periods of resiliency, during which they may feel able to engage in risky behaviors with relative safety.

Chapter 6

1. Almost half of the women I interviewed knew of or had visited a traditional healer at some time in their lives for these issues. Even though the work of Pima medicine men was long condemned by missionaries as a heathen, "primitive" practice, an estimated 150 Pima (both Akimel and Tohono O'odham) shamans were still in practice in 1974 (Bahr 1974; Heard 1938). I have been able to identify only one Akimel O'odham healer who is, reportedly, in training under a Tohono O'odham shaman. This information is certainly sensitive, difficult to access by non-Indians, and not the focus of my work. Nevertheless, I heard enough about traditional healers to demonstrate that traditional healing methods, including medicines, prayers, salves, and charms, are still recognized if not widely used by Pimas. It is the elders who employ healers and traditional medicines most often, indicating the continued decline of these practices in younger generations. Biomedicine has for decades been, simply, "medicine" to Pimas and is the only form of healing known to many Pima children.

2. A most important feature of the biomedical paradigm that is foreign to historic Native American healing practices is the segregation of illness from the home to the isolation of a hospital. Several historic developments contributed to this, including: increasing urbanization and industrialization in which work is more typically performed away from home on a schedule that does not permit care for ill family members; increased attention to the efficient use of physician time by scheduling multiple patients in a hospital setting rather than travel from home to home; and decreasing family size, which negatively impacted income and made home care more costly through missed work (Foucault 1973; Gordon 1988; Thomas 1983). As biological and physiological information became esoteric to biomedicine and its licensed practitioners, other forms of knowledge were excluded from officially sanctioned practice. Lay and indigenous forms of health knowledge struggle against this exclusionary pressure from biomedicine in the United States.

Another feature of biomedicine that is foreign to more traditional forms of care is its attachment to technology and science. Biomedicine is in many contexts synonymous with technologically produced care. Technology has freed biomedicine from other nonscientific or nontechnological influences on health, such as the social, economic, or political influences.

Medical anthropologists have attempted to reinsert the complexities of class action and consciousness (Waitzkin and Waterman 1974), non-agentive forms of hegemony (Comaroff and Comaroff 1992), forms of resistance, and cultural constructions of personhood (Mishler 1981; Stepan 1993) into studies and practice of biomedicine. Theories of political economy based on dependency and the global capitalist market have also gained supporters in medical anthropology because they emphasize, rather than ignore, the "social origins of disease, structural constraints on health, and international relations of domination and subordination" (Morgan 1987:147).

3. Other such terms that were sometimes confused or had multiple meanings included: *left* and *right* as directional markers; *traditional* as a reference to personality types, housing, etc.; *culture*; and various terms referring to weight, such as *chunky*.

Chapter 7

1. The Quest program is a youth education program at Gila River that is based in tribal elementary schools, where children learn the basics of good nutrition and exercise, as well as the risks and complications of diabetes. The Strong Heart Study, aimed at understanding and preventing heart disease, is also active at Gila River, as is the new Look Ahead project, designed to determine the long-term health effects of weight loss in people with type 2 diabetes. The Diabetes Prevention Project of the NIDDKD, the one so well attended and liked by Pimas with whom I spoke, employed tribal members and improved long-term participation in diet and exercise programs. The program sent health educators into the neighborhoods, not only to talk with participants, but to eat and exercise *with* them on a regular basis. The Pima Action/Pima Pride study was another that found, with ample support and participatory interventions, that several improvements in diabetic health could be measured. And there are many programs I have not mentioned that are likewise meeting with programmatic success. Nevertheless, despite all this "success," diabetes incidence rates continue to rise, because the bulk of these programs are aimed only at personal change—not at community transformation.

Chapter 8

1. A blood glucose reading of 900 is very rare and typically puts a person into a coma. I have, however, heard several anecdotal cases of readings this high at Gila River.

Chapter 9

1. Robert Hackenberg, in a more detailed discussion of the development of Piman economy in the twentieth century, describes their transition in farming as being from "edible subsistence" to "commercial subsistence" (1955a: 89), terms which more accurately reflect the absence of real profit achieved by Piman farmers after colonization.

2. The land title was held in trust for 25 years, after which it was transferred to the Indian owner.

3. The Civilian Conservation Corps–Indian Division and the Emergency Conservation Corps provided jobs to many Pimas during World War II, when the reservation served as a relocation center for Japanese Americans. Increasing emigration from the reservation to wage labor jobs in Phoenix contributed to a growing diversity of moral, economic, material, and religious values in the Pima.

4. Likewise, women may take elements of biomedical knowledge and use it selectively to exert some agency on what might otherwise be an uncontrollable illness (Nichter 1998).

5. Marie Chona, a Papago (Tohono O'odham) Indian woman, discussed this in her autobiography, cowritten with Ruth Underhill (1979).

6. Community member knowledge and opinion of this research vary. While many Pimas have participated in various NIH research projects, the medical findings are not well understood by community members. Reports of findings are made in each of the seven districts, but these district meetings are attended by only a very small fraction of the population. Some see this type of research as exploitative (see *Arizona Republic,* Oct. 31–Nov. 2, 1999), while others are appreciative of these clinical trials as providing greater understanding and, in particular, medications and treatment for diabetes and its complications.

Chapter 10

1. The World Health Organization classifies South Asians as obese at a lower BMI (= 25).

Chapter 13

1. Tricia and every other woman who had received visits from the field nurse raved about the nurse and the format of those visits. They shared more information, perhaps because they were more comfortable, perhaps because the setting made it easier for her to remember her questions and problems, probably a combination of factors. The relationship with the field nurse is a more cooperative one, a less power-distant one, and one that is reliably more

personal and intimate—for obvious reasons. Doctors on this reservation do a good job by most reports, treating their patients respectfully and with care and concern. But those appointments are relatively short and in a hospital or clinic setting. The field nurse bypasses those barriers and, at the cost of seeing fewer patients, makes a greater and lasting impact on a few.

2. This is a fictitious scenario compiled from field notes and quotes collected as part of the ethnographic study described in this paper. Features of the scenario, such as Stephanie's age, the number of children, and her experience of screening and interpreting the results, are typical.

Chapter 14

1. New York City's famous public health champion, Hermann Biggs, used just such measures to exile an immigrant Irish cook, infectious with *Salmonella typhi,* to an island in New York's East River. Typhoid Mary was quarantined there for the rest of her life (Garrett 2001).

2. The very principles guiding biomedical ethics direct physicians to: (1) do good (beneficence); (2) do no harm (nonmaleficence); (3) respect patient autonomy; and (4) be just or promote justice in the delivery of care. A literary and social explosion has occurred in recent decades as these four principles have come into conflict over such dilemmas as: the removal of feeding tubes from patients in a persistent vegetative state; the question of abortion; and the use of fetal tissue in genetic research. The responsibilities of physicians to patients with GDM may also conflict with competing needs of the woman, the fetus, and even the genetic heritage of the Pima people.

Bibliography

American Diabetes Association

1998   Economic consequences of diabetes mellitus in the U.S. in 1997. *Diabetes Care* 21(2):296–320.

2000   Gestational diabetes mellitus. *Diabetes Care* 23(suppl. 1):577–579.

2002   Native Americans and Diabetes. Electronic document http://www .diabetes.org/communityprograms-and-localevents/nativeamericans.jsp, accessed December 15, 2005.

2003   Economic costs of diabetes in the U.S. in 2002. *Diabetes Care* 26(3):917–932.

2004   Gestational diabetes mellitus (position statement). *Diabetes Care* 27(1):S88–S90.

Acton, Kelly J., Nilka Rios Burrows, Kelly Moore, Linda Querec, Linda S. Geiss, and Michael M. Engelgau

2002   Trends in diabetes prevalence among American Indian and Alaska Native children, adolescents, and young adults. *American Journal of Public Health* 92(9):1485–1490.

Adler, Nancy E., Thomas Boyce, Margaret A. Chesney, Sheldon Cohen, Susan Folkman, Robert L. Kahn, and S. Leonard Syme

1994   Socioeconomic status and health: The challenge of the gradient. *American Psychologist* 49:15–24.

Amos, A. F., Daniel J. McCarty, and Paul Z. Zimmet

1997   The rising global burden of diabetes and its complications: Estimates and projections to the year 2010. *Diabetic Medicine* 14 (suppl. 5):S1–S85.

Anderson, Ross E., Shawn C. Franckowiak, Julia Snyder, Susan J. Bartlett, and Kevin R. Fontaine

1998   Can inexpensive signs encourage the use of stairs? Results from a community intervention. *Annals of Internal Medicine* 129(5):363–369.

Baer, Hans A., Merrill Singer, and Ida Susser

1997   *Medical Anthropology and the World System: A Critical Perspective.* Westport, CT: Bergin and Garvey.

Bahr, Donald M.

1974   *Piman Shamanism and Staying Sickness.* Juan Gregorio, shaman. David I. Lopez, interpreter. Albert Alvarez, editor. Tucson: University of Arizona Press.

Bahr, Donald M., Juan Smith, William Smith Allison, and Julian Hayden
  1994   *The Short, Swift Time of Gods on Earth: The Hohokam Chronicles.*
          Berkeley: University of California Press.
Bahti, Tom, and Mark Bahti
  1997   *Southwestern Indian Tribes.* Las Vegas: KC Publications.
Baker, Paul T., Joel M. Hanna, and Thelma S. Baker (editors)
  1986   *The Changing Samoans: Behavior and Health in Transition.* Oxford:
          Oxford University Press.
Barefoot, John C., Kimberly E. Maynard, Jean C. Beckham, Beverly H. Brum-
mett, Karen Hooker, and Ilene C. Siegler
  1998   Trust, health, and longevity. *Journal of Behavorial Medicine* 21(6):
          517–526.
Beckles, Gloria L., Michael M. Engelgau, K. M. Venkat Narayan, William H.
Herman, Ronald E. Aubert, and David R. Williamson
  1998   Population-based assessment of the level of care among adults
          with diabetes in the U.S. *Diabetes Care* 21(9):1432–1438.
Benyshek, Daniel C., John F. Martin, and Carol C. Johnston
  2001   A reconsideration of the origins of the type 2 diabetes epidemic
          among Native Americans and the implications for intervention
          policy. *Medical Anthropology* 20(1):25–64.
Berg, Marc, and Annemarie Mol (editors)
  1998   *Differences in Medicine: Unraveling Practices, Techniques, and Bodies.*
          Durham, NC: Duke University Press.
Bertoni, Alain G., Julie S. Krop, Gerard F. Anderson, and Frederick L. Brancati
  2002   Diabetes-related morbidity and mortality in a national sample of
          U.S. elders. *Diabetes Care* 25(3):471–475.
Bertoni, Alain G., Sharon H. Saydah, and Frederick L. Brancati
  2001   Diabetes and the risk of infection-related mortality in the U.S.
          Diabetes Care 24(6):1044.
Bindon, James R., and P. T. Baker
  1985   Modernization, migration and obesity among Samoan adults. *An-
          nals of Human Biology* 12:67–76.
Birungi, Harriet
  1998   Injections and self-help: Risk and trust in Ugandan health care.
          Social Science Medicine 47:1455–1462.
Bissell, Paul, Carl R. May, Peter R. Noyce
  2004   From compliance to concordance: Barriers to accomplishing a re-
          framed model of health care interactions. *Social Science & Medicine*
          58:851–862.
Bloomgarden, Zachary T.
  2000   Obesity and diabetes. *Diabetes Care* 23(10):1584–1590.
  2003   Prevention of obesity and diabetes. *Diabetes Care* 26(11):3172–
          3178.

Blumhagen, Dan

    1980   Hyper-tension: A folk illness with a medical name. *Culture, Medicine and Psychiatry* 4:197–227.

Bonomo, Matteo, Maria Luisa Gandini, Arturo Mastropasqua, Cristina Begher, Umberto Valentini, David Faden, and Alberto Morabito

    1998   Which cutoff level should be used in screening for glucose intolerance in pregnancy? *American Journal of Obstetrics & Gynecology* 179:179–185.

Boyle, James P., Amanda A. Honeycutt, K. M. Venkat Narayan, Thomas J. Hoerger, Linda S. Geiss, Hong Chen, and Theodore J. Thompson

    2001   Projection of diabetes burden through 2050: Impact of changing demography and disease prevalence in the U.S. *Diabetes Care* 24: 1936–1940.

Brancati, Frederick L., Paul K. Whelton, Lewis H. Kuller, and Michael J. Klag

    1996   Diabetes mellitus, race and socioeconomic status. *Annals of Epidemiology* 6(1):67–73.

Broussard, Brenda A., Mary Ann Bass, and M. Yvonne Jackson

    1982   Reasons for diabetic diet noncompliance among Cherokee Indians. *Journal of Nutrition Education* 14(2):56–57.

Brown, Sharon A., Ronald B. Harrist, Evangelina T. Villagomez, Mario Segura, Sara A. Barton, and Craig L. Hanis

    2000   Gender and treatment differences in knowledge, health beliefs, and metabolic control in Mexican Americans with type 2 diabetes. *Diabetes Educator* 26(3):425–438.

Brown, Tammy, Charlton Wilson, Kelly Moore, Lorraine Valdez, Cheryl Wilson, Gilliland Susan, and Kelly Acton

    2003   Temporal trends in obesity among American Indian/Alaska Native (AI/AN) people with diabetes. *Diabetes* 52(6):A214–16.

Brownell, K. G., Albert J. Stunkard, and J. M. Albaum

    1980   Evaluation and modification of exercise patterns in the natural environment. *American Journal of Psychiatry* 137:1540–1545.

Browner, Carole H., and Nancy Ann Press

    1997   The production of authoritative knowledge in American prenatal care. In *Childbirth and Authoritative Knowledge: Cross-Cultural Perspectives*, edited by Robbie Davis-Floyd and Carolyn F. Sargent, 141–156. Berkeley: University of California Press.

Browner, Carole H., and Carolyn F. Sargent

    1996   Anthropology and studies of human reproduction. In *Medical Anthropology: Contemporary Theory and Method*, rev. ed., edited by Carolyn F. Sargent and Thomas M. Johnson. Westport, CT: Praeger.

Buzzard, Marilyn

    1998   24-Hour dietary recall and food record methods. In *Nutritional*

Epidemiology, 2nd ed., edited by Walter Willett, 50–73. New York: Oxford University Press.

Campbell, Paul R.
1996 *Population projections of the United States by age, sex, race, and Hispanic origin: 1995 to 2050.* U.S. Bureau of the Census, Population Division, PPL-47. Washington, DC: U.S. Government Printing Office.

Canby, William C. Jr.
1988 *American Indian Law in a Nutshell.* 2nd ed. St. Paul, MN: West.

Capps, Lisa, and Elinor Ochs
1995 *Constructing Panic: The Discourse of Agoraphobia.* Cambridge: Harvard University Press.

Caprio, Sonia
2003 Obesity and type 2 diabetes: The twin epidemic. *Diabetes Spectrum* 16(4):230.

Caro, J. Jaime, Alexandra J. Ward, and Judith A. O'Brien
2002 Lifetime costs of complications resulting from type 2 diabetes in the U.S. *Diabetes Care* 25:476–481.

Carter, Janette S., Jacqueline A. Pugh, and Ana Monterrosa
1996 Non-insulin-dependent diabetes mellitus in minorities in the United States. *Annals of Internal Medicine* 125:221–232.

Case Management Advisor
2002 Noncompliance is biggest problem in diabetes CM: Patients find it hard to change their lifestyles. *Case Management Advisor* 12(11): 126–127.

Castetter, Edward F., and Willis H. Bell
1942 Early basis of Piman subsistence. In *Pima and Papago Indian Agriculture,* edited by Edward F. Castetter and Willis H. Bell, 28–53. Albuquerque: University of New Mexico Press.

Cavalli-Sforza, L. Tommaso, A. Rosman, Annette S. de Boer, and Ian Darnton-Hill
1996 Nutritional aspects of changes in disease patterns in the Western Pacific Region. *Bulletin of the World Health Organization* 74:307–318.

Celik, Yusuf, and David R. Hotchkiss
2000 The socio-economic determinants of maternal health care utilization in Turkey. *Social Science & Medicine* 50:1797–1806.

Charron-Prochownik, Denise
2000 Teach early and often. *Diabetes Forecast.* January:71–72.

Cheadle, A., B. M. Psaty, P. Diehr, T. Koepsell, E. Wagner, S. Curry, and A. Kristal
1995 Evaluating community-based nutrition programs: Comparing grocery store and individual-level survey measures of program impact. *Preventive Medicine* 24:71–79.

Chin, Marshall H., Steven B. Auerbach, Sandy Cook, James Harrison, Julie Koppert, Lei Jin, Fay Thiel, Theodore Karrison, Anita Harrand, Cindy T. Schaefer, Herbert T. Takashima, and Wylie McNabb
    2000   Quality of diabetes care in community health centers. *American Journal of Public Health* 90:431–434.

Chin-Hong, Peter V., and Stephen T. McGarvey
    1996   Lifestyle incongruity and adult blood pressure in Western Samoa. *Psychosomatic Medicine* 58(2):130–137.

Cohen, Marlene Zichi, Toni Tripp-Reimer, Christopher Smith, Bernard Sorofman, and Sonja Lively
    1994   Explanatory models of diabetes: Patient practitioner variation. *Social Science & Medicine* 38(1):59–66.

Comaroff, Jean, and John Comaroff
    1992   Bodily reform as historical practice. In *Ethnography and the Historical Imagination,* edited by John Comaroff and Jean Comaroff, 69–91. Boulder, CO: Westview Press.

Corcoy, Rosa, Apolonia Garcia-Patterson, Merce Albareda, and Alberto De Leiva
    2000   Poor performance of American Diabetes Association criteria in women with gestational diabetes. *Diabetes Care* 23:430–431.

Coyne, J. C., C. Wortman, and D. Lehman
    1988   The other side of support: Emotional overinvolvement and miscarried helping. In *Marshaling Social Support: Formats, Processes and Effects,* edited by Benjamin H. Gottlieb, 309–330. Newbury Park, CA: Sage.

Dabelea, Dana, Robert L. Hanson, Peter H. Bennett, Janine Roumain, William C. Knowler, and David J. Pettitt
    1998   Increasing prevalence of type 2 diabetes in American Indian children. *Diabetologia* 41:904–910.

Dabelea, Dana, Robert L. Hanson, Robert S. Lindsay, David J. Pettitt, Giuseppina Imperatore, Momin M. Gabir, Janine Roumain, Peter H. Bennett, and William C. Knowler
    2000   Intrauterine exposure to diabetes conveys risks for type 2 diabetes and obesity: A study of discordant sibships. *Diabetes* 49:2208–2211.

Daniel, Mark, Lawrence W. Green, Stephen A. Marion, Diane Gamble, Carol P. Herbert, Clyde Hertzman, and Sam B. Sheps
    1999   Effectiveness of community-directed diabetes prevention and control in a rural Aboriginal population in British Columbia, Canada. *Social Science & Medicine* 48:815–832.

Davis-Floyd, Robbie E., and Carolyn F. Sargent
    1997   *Childbirth and Authoritative Knowledge: Cross-Cultural Perspectives.* Berkeley: University of California Press.

Daviss, Betty-Anne
   1997   Heeding warnings from the canary, the whale, and the Inuit: A
          framework for analyzing competing types of knowledge about
          childbirth. In *Childbirth and Authoritative Knowledge: Cross-Cultural
          Perspectives,* edited by Robbie E. Davis-Floyd and Carolyn F. Sar-
          gent, 441–473. Berkeley: University of California Press.
de Aguiar, Luiz Guilherme Kraemer, Haroldo José de Matos, and Marília de
Brito Gomes
   2001   Could fasting plasma glucose be used for screening high-risk out-
          patients for gestational diabetes mellitus? *Diabetes Care* 24:954–
          955.
Dean, Heather J., T. Kue Young, Bertha Flett, and Pauline Wood-Steiman
   1998   Screening for type 2 diabetes in Aboriginal children in northern
          Canada [letter]. *Lancet* 352:1523–1524.
Deloria, Vine Jr., and Clifford M. Lytle
   1998   *The Nations Within: The Past and Future of American Indian Sov-
          ereignty.* Austin: University of Texas Press.
Diabetes Prevention Program Research Group
   2002   Reduction in the incidence of type 2 diabetes with lifestyle inter-
          vention or Metformin. *New England Journal of Medicine* 346:393–
          403.
Dobyns, Henry F.
   1989   *The Pima-Maricopa.* New York: Chelsea House.
Dorner, G., and A. Mohnike
   1976   Further evidence for a predominantly maternal transmission of
          maturity-onset type diabetes. *Endokrinologie* 68(1):121–124.
Dressler, William W.
   1982   *Hypertension and Culture Change: Acculturation and Disease in the
          West Indies.* South Salem, NY: Redgrave.
   1985   Psychosomatic symptoms, stress, and modernization: A model.
          Culture, Medicine and Psychiatry 9:257–286.
   1987   The stress process in a Southern Black community: Implications
          for prevention research. *Human Organization* 46(3):211–220.
Dressler, William W., and James R. Bindon
   2000   The health consequences of cultural consonance: Cultural dimen-
          sions of lifestyle, social support, and arterial blood pressure in an
          African American community. *American Anthropologist* 102(2):
          244–260.
Drewnowski, A., and Barry M Popkin
   1997   The nutrition transition: New trends in the global diet. *Nutrition
          Reviews* 55:31–43.
Dunn, Stewart M., Linda J. Beeney, P. L. Hoskins, and John R. Turtle
   1990   Knowledge and attitude change as predictors of metabolic im-

provement in diabetes education. *Social Science & Medicine* 31: 1135–1141.

El-Kebbi, Imad M., Curtiss B. Cook, David C. Ziemer, Christopher D. Miller, Daniel L. Gallina, and Lawrence S. Phillips
    2003   Association of younger age with poor glycemic control and obesity in urban African Americans with type 2 diabetes. *Archives of Internal Medicine* 163:69–75.

Elder, Nancy C., and John Muench
    2000   Diabetes care as public health. *Journal of Family Practice* 49:513.

Elliot, Susan J.
    1995   Psychosocial stress, women and heart health: A critical review. *Social Science & Medicine* 40(1):105–115.

Ellison, R. Curtis, A. L. Capper, R. J. Goldberg, J. C. Witschi, and F. J. Stare
    1989   The environmental component: Changing school food service to promote cardiovascular health. *Health Education* 16(2):285–297.

Ellison, R. Curtis, A. L. Capper, and W. P. Stephenson
    1989   Effects on blood pressure of a decrease in sodium use in institutional food preparation: The Exeter-Andover Project. *Journal of Clinical Epidemiology* 42:201–208.

Epstein, L. H.
    1996   Family-based behavioural intervention for obese children. *International Journal of Obesity* 20(suppl. 1):S14–S21.

Expert Committee on the Diagnosis and Classification of Diabetes Mellitus
    1997   Report of the Expert Committee on the Diagnosis and Classification of Diabetes Mellitus. *Diabetes Care* 20:1183–1196.

Evaneshko, Veronica
    1994   Presenting complaints in a Navajo Indian diabetic population. In *Diabetes as a Disease of Civilization: The Impact of Culture Change on Indigenous Peoples,* edited by Jennie R. Joe and Robert S. Young, 357–378. New York: Mouton de Gruyter.

Fagan, Brian M.
    1995   *Ancient North America: The Archaeology of a Continent.* New York: Thames and Hudson.

Fagot-Campagna, Anne, David J. Pettitt, Michael M. Engelgau, Nilka Rios Burrows, Linda S. Geiss, Rodolfo Valdez, Gloria L. Beckles, Jinan Saaddine, Edward W. Gregg, David F. Williamson, and K. M. Venkat Narayan
    2000   Type 2 diabetes among North American children and adolescents: An epidemiological review and a public health perspective. *Journal of Pediatrics* 136:664–672.

Fagot-Campagna, Anne, Nilka Rios Burrows, and David F. Williamson
    1999   The public health epidemiology of type 2 diabetes in children and adolescents: A case study of American Indian adolescents in the Southwestern United States. *Clinica Chimica Acta* 286:81–95.

Fagot-Campagna, Anne, Jinan B. Saaddine, Katherine M. Flegal, and Gloria L. A. Beckles
  2001   Diabetes, impaired fasting glucose, and elevated HbA_{1c} in U.S. adolescents: The Third National Health and Nutrition Examination Survey. *Diabetes Care* 24:834–837.
Farmer, Paul
  1994   AIDS-Talk and the constitution of cultural models. *Social Science & Medicine* 38:801–809.
Ferzacca, Steve
  1990   Embodied morality: Diagnostics, clinical practice, and non-insulin-dependent diabetes mellitus (NIDDM). Paper delivered to a meeting of the Southwestern Anthropological Association, Tucson, 1990.
  1991   Foodways and the treatment of non-insulin-dependent diabetes mellitus (NIDDM): Food good for eating—good for thinkers. Unpublished paper in the possession of the author.
Flegal, Katherine M., Margaret D. Carroll, Cynthia L. Ogden, and Clifford L. Johnson
  2002   Prevalence and trends in obesity among U.S. adults, 1999–2000. *Journal of the American Medical Association* 288:1723–1727.
Fleming, Barbara B., Sheldon Greenfield, Michael M. Engelgau, Leonard M. Pogach, Steven B. Clauser, and Marian A. Parrott
  2001   The Diabetes Quality Improvement Project. *Diabetes Care* 24: 1815–1820.
Foucault, Michel
  1973   *The Birth of the Clinic: An Archaeology of Medical Perception.* New York: Vintage Books.
Franciosi, Monica, Fabio Pellegrini, Giorgia De Berardis, Maurizio Belfiglio, Donatella Cavaliere, Barbara Di Nardo, Sheldon Greenfield, Sherrie H. Kaplan, Michele Sacco, Gianni Tognoni, Miriam Valentini, and Antonio Nicolucci
  2001   The impact of blood glucose self-monitoring on metabolic control and quality of life in type 2 diabetic patients. *Diabetes Care* 24: 1870–1877.
Franz, Marion J. (editor)
  2001   *A Core Curriculum for Diabetes Education: Diabetes Management Therapies,* 4th ed. Chicago: American Association of Diabetes Educators.
Frazer, James George
  1922   *The Golden Bough: A Study in Magic and Religion.* New York: Macmillan.
Freeman, Joshua, and Ronald Loewe
  2000   Barriers to communication about diabetes mellitus: Patients' and physicians' different views of the disease. *Journal of Family Practice* 49:507–512.

Freinkel, Norbert
    1980   Of pregnancy and progeny. *Diabetes* 29:1023–1035.
French, S. A., R. W. Jeffery, M. Story, P. Hannan, and M. P. Snyder
    1997   A pricing strategy to promote low-fat snack choices through vend-
            ing machines. *American Journal of Public Health* 87:849–851.
Garcia-Smith, Dianna
    1994   The Gila River Diabetes Prevention Model. In *Diabetes as a Disease
            of Civilization: The Impact of Culture Change on Indigenous Peoples*,
            edited by Jennie R. Joe and Robert S. Young, 471–494. New York:
            Mouton de Gruyter.
Garfield, Sanford A., Saul Malozowski, Marshall H. Chin, K. M. Venkat
Narayan, Russell E. Glasgow, Lawrence W. Green, Roland Hiss, Harlan M.
Krumholz, and The Diabetes Mellitus Interagency Coordinating Committee
(DMICC) Translation Conference Working Group
    2003   Considerations for diabetes translational research in real-world
            settings. *Diabetes Care* 26(9):2670–2674.
Garrett, Laurie
    2001   *Betrayal of Trust: The Collapse of Global Public Health*. New York:
            Hyperion Press.
Garro, Linda C.
    1994   Narrative representations of chronic illness experience: Cultural
            models of illness, mind, and body in stories concerning the tem-
            poromandibular joint (TMJ). *Social Science & Medicine* 18:775–
            788.
Geiss, Linda S. (editor)
    1999   *Diabetes Surveillance, 1999*. Atlanta: Centers for Disease Control
            and Prevention, U.S. Department of Health and Human Services.
Gertler, Paul, M. Omar Rahman, Chris Feifer, and Deanna Ashley
    1993   Determinants of pregnancy outcomes and targeting of maternal
            health services in Jamaica. *Social Science & Medicine* 37:199–211.
Gifford, Sandra M.
    1986   The meaning of lumps: A case study of the ambiguities of risk. In
            *Anthropology and Epidemiology: Interdisciplinary Approaches to the
            Study of Health and Disease*, edited by Craig R. Janes, 213–246.
            Norwell, MA: Kluwer Academic.
Ginsburg, Faye D., and Rayna Rapp (editors)
    1995   *Conceiving the New World Order: The Global Politics of Reproduction*.
            Los Angeles: University of California Press.
Glasgow, Russell, Paul Nutting, Diane King, Geoffrey Williams, Candace
Nelson, Bridget Gaglio, Hilarea Amthauer, and Alanna-Kulchak Rahm
    2003   Variation in perceived competence and patient satisfaction: Rela-
            tionship to autonomy support from physicians. *Diabetes* 52:A39.

Gohdes, Dorothy, and Kelly Acton
    2000   Diabetes mellitus and its complications. In *American Indian Health: Innovations in Health Care, Promotion, and Policy,* edited by Everett R. Rhoades, 221–243. Baltimore: Johns Hopkins University Press.

Goldberg-Ambrose, Carole
    1994   Of Native Americans and tribal members: The impact of law on Indian group life. *Law and Society Review* 28(5):1123–1147.

Good, Byron J.
    1977   The heart of what's the matter: The semantics of illness in Iran. *Cultural Medical Psychiatry* 1:25–58.

Good, Byron J., and Mary-Jo Del Vecchio Good
    1994   In the subjunctive mode: Epilepsy narratives in Turkey. *Social Science & Medicine* 38:835–842.

Goodenough, Ward H.
    1976   Multiculturalism as the normal human experience. *Anthropology and Education Quarterly* 7(4):4–6.

Gordon, Deborah R.
    1988   Tenacious assumptions in Western medicine. In *Biomedicine Examined,* edited by Margaret Lock and Deborah R. Gordon, 19–56. Dordrecht, The Netherlands: Kluwer Academic.

Gramsci, Antonio
    1971   *Selections from the Prison Notebooks of Antonio Gramsci.* Edited and translated by Quintin Hoare and Geoffrey Nowell Smith. New York: International Publishers.

Green, James R., I. G. Pawson, L. B. Schumacher, J. Perry, and N. Kretchmer
    1990   Glucose tolerance in pregnancy: Ethnic variation and influence of body habitus. *American Journal of Obstetrics & Gynecology* 163:86–92.

Guerrant, Richard L., M. Auxiliadora de Souza, and Marilyn K. Nations
    1996   Part 1: The social and cultural context of disease, its morbidity, and its mortality, at the edge of development. In *At the Edge of Development: Health Crises in a Transitional Society,* edited by Richard L. Guerrant, M. Auxiliadora de Souza, and Marilyn K. Nations, 1–88. Durham, NC: Carolina Academic Press.

Gulli, G., E. Ferrannini, M. Stern, S. Haffner, and R. A. DeFronzo
    1992   The metabolic profile of NIDDM is fully established in glucose-tolerant offspring of two Mexican-American NIDDM parents. *Diabetes* 41:1575–1586.

Hackenberg, Robert A.
    1955a A brief history of the Gila River Reservation. In *Economic and Political Change Among the Gila River Pima Indians,* a report to the John Hay Whitney Foundation, 11–94. BER Archives, Arizona State Museum, University of Arizona, Tucson.

1955b   *Economic and Political Change among the Gila River Pima Indians.* A report to the John Hay Whitney Foundation. BER Archives, Arizona State Museum, University of Arizona, Tucson.

Historic America Engineering Record

1996   Agricultural development and economic consequences of SCIP. In *Historic America Engineering Record: San Carlos Irrigation Project.*

Hagey, Rebecca

1984   The phenomenon, the explanations and the responses: Metaphors surrounding diabetes in urban Canadian Indians. *Social Science & Medicine* 18:265–272.

1989   The native diabetes program: Rhetorical process and praxis. *Medical Anthropology* 12:7–33.

Hahn, Robert

1995   Anthropology and epidemiology: One logic or two? In *Sickness and Healing: An Anthropological Perspective,* edited by Robert Hahn, 99–128. New Haven, CT: Yale University Press.

Hall, Teri R., Martin E. Hickey, and Terry B. Young

1992   Evidence for recent increases in obesity and non-insulin-dependent diabetes mellitus in a Navajo community. *American Journal of Human Biology* 4:547–553.

Hampson, Sarah E., Russell E. Glasgow, and Lyn S. Foster

1995   Personal models of diabetes among older adults: Relationship of self-management and other variables. *Diabetes Educator* 21:300–307.

Hanley, Anthony J. G., Stewart B. Harris, Joel Gittelsohn, Thomas M. S. Wolever, Brit Saksvig, and Bernard Zinman

2000   Overweight among children and adolescents in a Native Canadian community: Prevalence and associated factors. *American Journal of Clinical Nutrition* 71:693–700.

Hanna, Joel M., and Maureen H. Fitzgerald

1993   Acculturation and symptoms: A comparative study of reported health symptoms in three Samoan communities. *Social Science & Medicine* 36:1169–1180.

Hardy, Kevin J., Sarah V. O'Brien, and Niall J. Furlong

2001   Information given to patients before appointments and its effect on non-attendance rate. *British Medical Journal* 323:1298–1300.

Harjo, Suzan Shown

2005   Harjo: My New Year's resolution: No more fat "Indian" food. *Indian Country Today*, January 26.

Harris, Maureen I.

1998   Diabetes in America: Epidemiology and scope of the problem. *Diabetes Care* 21(suppl. 3):C11–C14.

Harris, Maureen I., Katherine Flegal, Catherine C. Cowie, Mark S. Eberhardt, David E. Goldstein, Randie R. Little, Hsiao-MeiWiedmeyer, and Danita D. Byrd-Holt
  1998   Prevalence of diabetes, impaired fasting glucose, and impaired glucose tolerance in U.S. adults: The Third National Health and Nutrition Examination Survey, 1988–1994. *Diabetes Care* 21: 518–524.

Hauptman, Laurence M.
  1994   Indian Reorganization Act. In *Native America in the Twentieth Century: An encyclopedia,* 262–264. New York: Garland Publishing.

Hayes, Michael V.
  1991   The risk approach: Unassailable logic. *Social Science & Medicine* 33:55–70.

Heard, Marvin E.
  1938   Three Centuries of Formal and Informal Education Influences and Development among the Pima Indians. Thesis, University of Arizona.

Heurtin-Roberts, Suzanne
  1993   "High-Pertension"—The uses of a chronic folk illness for personal adaptation. *Social Science & Medicine* 37:285–294.

Hill, J., and J. Peters
  1998   Environmental contributions to the obesity epidemic. *Science* 280(s1371–s1374).

Hill, Mary Anne
  1997   The curse of frybread: The diabetes epidemic in Indian country. *Winds of Change* 12(3):26–31.

Hoffman-Goetz, Laurie, and Sherry L. Mills
  1998   Cultural barriers to cancer screening among African American Women: A critical review of the qualitative literature. *Women's Health: Research on Gender, Behavior, and Policy* 3(3–4):183–201.

Hunt, Linda M., Nedal H. Arar, and Anne C. Larme
  1998   Contrasting patient and practitioner perspectives in type 2 diabetes management. *Western Journal of Nursing Research* 20:656–682.

Hunt, Linda M., Miguel A. Valenzuela, and Jacqueline A. Pugh
  1998   ¿Porque me tocó a mí? Mexican American diabetes patients' causal stories and their relationship to treatment behaviors. *Social Science & Medicine* 46:959–969.

Hunter, John M.
  1992   Elephantiasis: A disease of development in north east Ghana. *Social Science & Medicine* 35(5):627–649.

Hunter, John M., Luis Rey, and David Scott
  1983   Man-made lakes—man-made diseases. *World Health Forum* 4:177–182.

Hymes, Dell H.

1967   *Studies in Southwestern Ethnolinguistics: Meaning and History in the Languages of the American Southwest*. The Hague, Paris: Mouton.

IDEA Health & Fitness Association

2001   U.S. sees major increase in diabetes. *Health and Fitness Source* 19(1):18.

International Diabetes Federation

2001   *Diabetes Atlas 2000*. Brussels: IDF.

Jackson, M. Yvonne

1994   Diet, culture and diabetes. In *Diabetes as a Disease of Civilization: The Impact of Culture Change on Indigenous Peoples*, edited by Jennie R. Joe and Robert S. Young, 381–406. Berlin: Mouton de Gruyter.

Jakicic, John M., Rena R. Wing, B. A. Butler, and Robert W. Jeffery

1997   The relationship between presence of exercise equipment in the home and physical activity level. *American Journal of Health Promotion* 11:363–365.

Janes, Craig R.

1990   Migration, changing gender roles and stress: The Samoan case. *Medical Anthropology* 12:217–248.

Jarrett, R. J.

1997   Should we screen for gestational diabetes? *British Medical Journal* 315:736–737.

Jeffery, Robert W., Simone A. French, C. Raether, and J. E. Baxter

1994   An environmental intervention to increase fruit and salad purchases in a cafeteria. *Preventive Medicine* 23:788–792.

Joe, Jennie R.

1994   Perceptions of diabetes by Indian adolescents. In *Diabetes as a Disease of Civilization: The Impact of Culture Change on Indigenous Peoples*, edited by Jennie R. Joe and Robert S. Young, 329–356. New York: Mouton de Gruyter.

Joe, Jennie R., and Robert S. Young (editors)

1994   *Diabetes as a Disease of Civilization: The Impact of Culture Change on Indigenous Peoples*. New York: Mouton de Gruyter.

Joos, Sandra K., William H. Mueller, Craig L. Hanis, and William J. Schull

1984   Diabetes alert study: Weight history and upper body obesity in diabetic and non-diabetic Mexican American adults. *Annals of Human Biology* 11(2):167–171.

Jordan, Brigitte

1997   Authoritative knowledge and its construction. In *Childbirth and Authoritative Knowledge: Cross-Cultural Perspectives*, edited by Robbie Davis-Floyd and Carolyn F. Sargent, 55–79. Berkeley: University of California Press.

1993   *Birth in Four Cultures: A Cross-Cultural Investigation of Childbirth in Yucatan, Holland, Sweden and the United States,* 4th ed. Prospect Heights, IL: Waveland Press.

Justice, James W.

1994   The history of diabetes in the Desert People. In *Diabetes as a Disease of Civilization: The Impact of Culture Change on Indigenous Peoples,* edited by Jennie R. Joe and Robert S. Young, 69–127. New York: Mouton de Gruyter.

Juutinen, Jaana, Anna-Liisa Hartikainen, Risto Bloigu, and Juha S. Tapanainen

2000   A retrospective study on 435 women with gestational diabetes. *Diabetes Care* 23:1858–1859.

Katz, Jay

1984   *The Silent World of Doctor and Patient.* New York: Free Press.

Kavanagh, Anne M., and Dorothy H. Broom

1998   Embodied risk: My body myself? *Social Science & Medicine* 46:437–444.

Kitzmiller, John L., T. A. Buchanan, S. Kjos, C. A. Combs, and R. E. Ratner

1996   Pre-conception care of diabetes, congenital malformations, and spontaneous abortions. *Diabetes Care* 19:514–541.

Kleinman, Arthur

1985   Interpreting illness experience and clinical meanings: How I see clinically applied anthropology. *Medical Anthropology Quarterly* 16 (3):69–71.

Knowler, William C., Elizabeth Barrett-Connor, Sarah E. Fowler, Richard F. Hamman, John M. Lachin, Elizabeth A. Walker, and David M. Nathan

2002   Reduction in the incidence of type 2 diabetes with lifestyle intervention or metformin. *New England Journal of Medicine* 346:393–403.

Knowler, William C., David J. Pettitt, Peter H. Bennett, and R. C. Williams

1983   Diabetes mellitus in the Pima Indians: Genetic and evolutionary considerations. *American Journal of Physical Anthropology* 62:107–114.

Knowler, William C., David J. Pettitt, Mohammed F. Saad, and Peter H. Bennett

1990   Diabetes mellitus in the Pima Indians: Incidence, risk factors and pathogenesis. *Diabetes/Metabolism Reviews* 6(1):1–27.

Knowler, William C., David J. Pettitt, Mohammed F. Saad, Marie-Aline Charles, Robert G. Nelson, Barbara V. Howard, Clifton Bogardus, and Peter H. Bennett

1991   Obesity in the Pima Indians: Its magnitude and relationship with diabetes. *American Journal of Clinical Nutrition* 53:1543S–1551S.

Kozak, David L.

1997   Surrendering to diabetes: An embodied response to perceptions of diabetes and death in the Gila River Indian community. *Omega* 35:347–359.

2005   Body Mass IMAGE (the Other BMI): Adding culture to the BMI equation. Paper presented to the meeting of the Society for Medical Anthropology, Santa Fe, March 5–9.

Kracht, Benjamin R.

1994   Diabetes among the Kiowa: An ethnohistorical perspective. In *Diabetes as a Disease of Civilization: The Impact of Culture Change on Indigenous Peoples,* edited by Jennie R. Joe and Robert S. Young, 147–167. New York: Mouton de Gruyter.

Kuczmarski, Robert J., Katherine M. Flegal, Stephen M. Campbell, and Clifford L. Johnson

1994   Increasing prevalence of overweight among U.S. adults. The National Health and Nutrition Examination Surveys, 1960 to 1991. *Journal of the American Medical Association* 272:205–211.

Kumanyika, Shiriki

1988   Obesity in Black women. *Epidemiological Review* 9:31–50.

1993   Special issues regarding obesity in minority populations. *Annals of Internal Medicine* 119:650–654.

Kunitz, Stephen J.

1983   The historical roots and ideological functions of disease concepts in three primary care specialties. *Historical Medicine Journal* 57: 412–431.

Kunstadter, Peter

1991   Social and behavioral factors in transmission and response to shigellosis. *Reviews of Infectious Diseases* 13(4):272–278.

Lang, Gretchen Chesley

1989   "Making sense" about diabetes: Dakota narratives of illness. *Medical Anthropology* 11:305–327.

1990   Talking about a new illness with the Dakota: Reflections on diabetes, food, and culture. In *Culture and the Anthropological Tradition,* edited by Robert H. Winthrop, 283–317. New York: University Press of America.

Lao, Terence T., and Lai-Fong Ho

2004   Impact of iron deficiency anemia on prevalence of gestational diabetes mellitus. *Diabetes Care* 27:650–656.

Larme, Anne C., and Jacqueline A. Pugh

1998   Attitudes of primary care providers toward diabetes: Barriers to guideline implementation. *Diabetes Care* 21(9):1391–1396.

2001   Evidence-based guidelines meet the real world. *Diabetes Care.* 24:1728–1733.

Lawson, Erma Jean, and Shireen Rajaram

1994   A transformed pregnancy: The psychosocial consequences of gestational diabetes. *Sociology of Health & Illness* 16:536–562.

Lazarus, Ellen J.

    1990   Falling through the cracks: Contradictions and barriers to care in a prenatal clinic. *Medical Anthropology* 12:269–287.

    1997   *What Do Women Want? Issues of Choice, Control, and Class in American Pregnancy and Childbirth.* Berkeley: University of California Press.

Lewando-Hundt, G., I. Shoham-Vardi, S. Beckerleg, I. Belmaker, S. Kassem, and A. A. Jaafar

    2001   Knowledge, action and resistance: The selective use of pre-natal screening among Bedouin women of the Negev, Israel. *Social Science & Medicine* 52:561–569.

Lewis, Gilbert

    1993   Concepts of health and illness in a Sepik society. In *Concepts of Health, Illness, and Disease: A Comparative Perspective,* edited by Caroline Currer and Meg Stacey, 119–135. Oxford: Berg.

Li, X., M. Quinones, M. Saad, I. Enriquez, X. Jimenez, R. de la Rosa, J. Cadenas, D. Bustos, J. Rotter, W. Hsueh, and H. Yang.

    2003   Pleiotropic genetic effects on insulin resistance and obesity in Mexican American families. *Diabetes* 52:A252–A254.

Lia-Hoagberg, Betty, Peter Rode, Catherine J. Skovholt, Charles N. Oberg, Cynthia Berg, Sara Mullett, and Thomas Choi

    1990   Barriers and motivators to prenatal care among low-income women. *Social Science & Medicine* 30(4):487–495.

Liburd, Leandris C., and Frank Vinicor

    2003   Rethinking diabetes prevention and control in racial and ethnic communities. *Journal of Public Health Management and Practice* 9(6):S74–S79.

Lieberman, Leslie Sue

    2000   Diabetes. In *The Cambridge History and Geography of Human Disease Project,* edited by Kenneth F. Kiple, 665–676. Cambridge: Cambridge University Press.

    2003   Dietary, evolutionary and modernizing influences on the prevalence of type 2 diabetes. *Annual Review of Nutrition* 23:345–377.

    2004   Diabetes mellitus and medical anthropology. In *Encyclopedia of Medical Anthropology: Health and Illness in the World's Cultures: 1. Topics,* edited by Carol R. Ember and Melvin Ember. New York: Kluwer Academic/Plenum Publishers.

Lieberman, Leslie Sue, Claudia K. Probart, and Nancy E. Schoenberg

    1999   Barriers to weight reduction among African-American women with type 2 diabetes. In *Third Conference of National Leaders in Women's Health Research: Health education in special populations.* Gainesville, FL: Health Sciences Center.

Lindsay, Robert S., Dana Dabelea, Janine Roumain, Robert Hanson, Peter H. Bennett, and William C. Knowler
  2000 Type 2 diabetes and low birth weight: The role of paternal inheritance in the association of low birth weight and diabetes. *Diabetes* 49:445–449.

Lipsman, Joshua
  1988 White man's medicine. In *Nation* March:401.

Lock, Margaret
  1989 Words of fear, words of power: Nerves and the awakening of political consciousness. *Medical Anthropology* 11:79–90.

Loustaunau, Martha O., and Elisa J. Sobo
  1997 *The Cultural Context of Health, Illness, and Medicine*. Westport, CT: Bergin and Garvey.

Magee, M. Scott, Carolyn E. Walden, Thomas J. Benedetti, and Robert H. Knopp
  1993 Influence of diagnostic criteria on the incidence of gestational diabetes and perinatal morbidity. *Journal of the American Medical Association* 269:609–615.

Maskarinec, Gertraud
  1997 Diabetes in Hawaii: Estimating prevalence from insurance claims data. *American Journal of Public Health* 87:1717–1720.

McKeown, Thomas
  1985 Looking at disease in the light of human development. *World Health Forum* 6:70–75.

Mead, Michael
  2004 Ten key facts about obesity in type 2 diabetes. *Diabetes and Primary Care* 5(4):158–161.

Mello, Giorgio, Elena Parretti, Riccardo Cioni, Roberto Lucchetti, Lucia Carignani, Elisabetta Martini, Federico Mecacci, Corrado Lagazio, and Monica Pratesi
  2003 The 75-gram glucose load in pregnancy: Relation between glucose levels and anthropometric characteristics of infants born to women with normal glucose metabolism. *Diabetes Care* 26(4): 1206–1210.

Michielutte, Robert, Penny C. Sharp, Mark B. Dignan, and Karen Blinson
  1994 Cultural issues in the development of cancer control programs for American Indian populations. *Journal of Health Care for the Poor and Underserved* 5(4):280–296.

Miller, William R., and Stephen Rollnick
  1991 *Motivational Interviewing*. New York: Guilford Press.

Mills, James L., L. Baker, and A. S. Goldman
  1979 Malformations in infants of diabetic mothers occur before the seventh gestational week: Implications for treatment. *Diabetes* 28:292–293.

Mishler, Elliot G., Lorna R. Amara-Singham, Stuart T. Hauser, Ramsay Liem,
Samuel D. Osherson, and Nancy E. Waxler
   1981   *Social Contexts of Health, Illness, and Patient Care.* Cambridge: Cam-
          bridge University Press.
Mokdad, Ali H., Earl S. Ford, Barbara A. Bowman, David E. Nelson, Michael
M. Engelgau, Frank Vinicor, and James S. Marks
   2000   Diabetes trends in the U.S.: 1990–1998. *Diabetes Care* 23:1278–
          1283.
   2001   The continuing increase of diabetes in the U.S. *Diabetes Care*
          24:412.
Montague, Carl T., and Stephen O'Rahilly
   2000   The perils of portliness: Causes and consequences of visceral
          adiposity. *Diabetes* 49:883–888.
Morgan, Lynn M.
   1987   Dependency theory in the political economy of health: An anthro-
          pological critique. *Medical Anthropology Quarterly* 1(2):131–151.
Mueller, William H., Sandra K. Joos, Craig L. Hanis, Anthony N. Zavaleta,
June Eichner, William J. Schull
   1984   The diabetes alert study: Growth, fatness, and fat patterning, ado-
          lescence through adulthood in Mexican Americans. *American Jour-
          nal of Physical Anthropology* 64:389–399.
Nabhan, Gary P.
   1992   *Gathering the Desert.* Tucson: University of Arizona Press.
Nabhan, Gary P., Charles W. Weber, and James W. Berry
   1985   Variations in compositions of Hopi Indian beans. *Ecology of Food
          and Nutrition* 16:135–152.
Nagel, Joane
   1996   *American Indian Ethnic Renewal: Red Power and the Resurgence of
          Identity and Culture.* New York: Oxford University Press.
Narayan, K. M. Venkat, M. Hoskin, David L. Kozak, A. M. Kriska, Robert L.
Hanson, David J. Pettitt, D. K. Nagi, Peter H. Bennett, and William C. Knowler
   1998   Randomized clinical trial of lifestyle interventions in Pima In-
          dians: A pilot study. *Diabetic Medicine* 15:66–72.
Narayan, K. M. Venkat, Corette Parker, Edward Gregg, Anne Fagot-Campagna,
Gloria Beckles, Ty Hartwell, Wendy Visscher, Steve Sorensen, and Michael
Engelgau
   1999   Relationship between patient satisfaction and preventive care
          practices among African-Americans with diabetes. *Diabetes* 48(5):
          SA198.
National Institute of Diabetes and Digestive and Kidney Diseases (NIDDKD)
   1996   *The Pima Indians: Pathfinders for Health.* Document no. NIH
          95-3821. Bethesda: NIDDKD, National Institutes of Health.

Neel, James V.

1962   Diabetes mellitus: A "thrifty" genotype rendered detrimental by "progress"? *American Journal of Human Genetics* 14:353–362.

1982   The thrifty genotype revisited. In *The Genetics of Diabetes Mellitus,* edited by J. Köbberling and R. Tattersall. New York: Academic Press.

Neiger, Ran, and Donald R. Coustan

1991   Are the current ACOG glucose tolerance test criteria sensitive enough? *Obstetrics & Gynecology* 78:1117–1120.

Neilson, D. R. Jr., R. N. Bolton, R. P. Prins, C. Mark III

1991   Glucose challenge testing in pregnancy. *American Journal of Obstetrics & Gynecology* 164:1673–1679.

Nestle, Marion

2002   *Food Politics: How the Food Industry Influences Nutrition and Health.* Berkeley: University of California Press.

Newman, Jeffrey M., Frank DeStefano, Sarah E. Valway, Robert R. German, and Ben Muneta

1993   Diabetes-associated mortality in Native Americans. *Diabetes Care* 16(1):297–299.

Nichter, Mark

1987   Kyasanur Forest Disease: An ethnography of a disease of development. *Political Ecology* 1:406–423.

1998   Vulnerability, prophylactic antibiotic use, harm reduction and the misguided appropriation of medical resources: The case of STDs in S. E. Asia. In *Seminar on Cultural Perspectives on Reproductive Health: Papers,* 1–38. Liège, Belgium: International Union for the Scientific Study of Population and The University of the Witwatersrand, Department of Community Health.

O'Neil, John D., and Patricia Leyland Kaufert

1995   Irniktakpunga! Sex determination and the Inuit struggle for birthing rights in Northern Canada. In *Conceiving the New World Order: The Global Politics of Reproduction,* edited by Faye D. Ginsburg and Rayna Rapp, 59–73. Los Angeles: University of California Press.

Olson, Brooke

1999   Applying medical anthropology: Developing diabetes education and prevention programs in American Indian cultures. *American Indian Culture and Research Journal* 23(3):185–203.

Oropesa, R. S., N. S. Landale, M. Inkley, and B. K. Gorman

2000   Prenatal care among Puerto Ricans on the United States mainland. *Social Science & Medicine* 51:1723–1739.

Ortiz, Alfonso

1973   The Gila River Piman water problem: An ethnohistorical account. In *The Changing Ways of Southwestern Indians: A Historic Perspective,* edited by Al H. Schroeder, New Mexico: Rio Grande Press.

Parker, Alex, Joanne Meyer, Steve Lewitzky, Jean S. Rennich, Gayun Chan, Jeffrey D. Thomas, Marju Orho-Melander, Mikko Lehtovirta, Carol Forsblom, Auli Hyrkkö, Martin Carlsson, Cecilia Lindgren, and Leif C. Groop
    2001   A gene conferring susceptibility to type 2 diabetes in conjunction with obesity is located on chromosome 18p11. *Diabetes* 50:675–680.

Parkin, T., and T. C. Skinnert
    2003   Discrepancies between patient and professionals recall and perception of an outpatient consultation. *Diabetic Medicine* 20:909–914.

Parsons, Talcott
    1971   Action systems and social systems. In Parsons, *The System of Modern Societies,* 4–8. Englewood Cliffs, NJ: Prentice-Hall.

Pearce, Tola Olu
    1993   Lay medical knowledge in an African context. In *Knowledge, Power and Practice: The Anthropology of Medicine in Everyday Life,* edited by Shirley Lindenbaum and Margaret Lock, 150–165. Berkeley: University of California Press.

Pearlin, Leonard I.
    1982   The social contexts of stress. In *Handbook of Stress,* edited by Leo Goldberger and Shlomo Breznitz. New York: Free Press.

Pendry, De Ann
    1998   Crossing borders with information and resources for the treatment of diabetes. In *The Survival of Families in Poverty in the United States/Mexico Border Region: Conference Proceedings,* edited by Manuel Ribeiro Ferreira and David M. Austin. Austin: The School of Social Work, University of Texas at Austin.

Persily, Cynthia Armstrong
    1996   Relationships between the perceived impact of gestational diabetes mellitus and treatment adherence. *JOGNN Clinical Studies* 25:601–607.

Perucchini, Daniele, Ursin Fischer, Giatgen A. Spinas, Renate Huch, Albert Huch, and Roger Lehmann
    1999   Using fasting plasma glucose concentrations to screen for gestational diabetes mellitus: Prospective population based study. *British Medical Journal* 319:812–815.

Pettitt, David J.
    2001   The 75-g Oral Glucose Tolerance Test in pregnancy. *Diabetes Care* 24:1129.

Pettitt, David J., Kirk A. Aleck, H. R. Baird, Michael J. Carraher, Peter H. Bennett, and William C. Knowler
    1988   Congenital susceptibility to NIDDM: Role of intrauterine environment. *Diabetes* 37:622–628.

Pettitt, David J., K. M. Venkat Narayan, Robert L. Hanson, and William C. Knowler

    1996   Incidence of diabetes mellitus in women following impaired glucose tolerance in pregnancy is lower than following impaired glucose tolerance in the non-pregnant state. *Diabetologia* 39:1334–1337.

Pettit, David J., Robert G. Nelson, Mohammed F. Saad, Peter H. Bennett, and William C. Knowler

    1993   Diabetes and obesity in the offspring of Pima Indian women with diabetes during pregnancy. *Diabetes Care* 16:310–314.

Pfaff, Christine

    1994   *The San Carlos Irrigation Project: An Historic Overview and Evaluation of Significance, Pinal County, Arizona.* Denver, CO: n.p.

Philips, Susan U.

    1983   *The Invisible Culture: Communication in Classroom and Community on the Warm Springs Indian Reservation.* Prospect Heights, IL: Waveland Press.

Pollock, Kristian

    1988   On the nature of social stress: Production of a modern mythology. *Social Science & Medicine* 26:381–392.

Popkin, Barry M.

    1998   The nutrition transition and its health implications in lower-income countries. *Public Health Nutrition* 1:5–21.

    2001   The nutrition transition and obesity in the developing world. *Journal of Nutrition* 131:871S–873S.

Price, R. Arlen, Marie-Aline Charles, David J. Pettitt, and William C. Knowler

    1993   Obesity in Pima Indians: Large increases among post–World War II birth cohorts. *American Journal of Physical Anthropology* 92:473–479.

Raghupathy, Shobana

    1996   Education and the use of maternal health care in Thailand. *Social Science & Medicine* 43:459–471.

Rapp, Rayna

    1988   Chromosomes and communication: The discourse of genetic counseling. *Medical Anthropology Quarterly* 2:143–157.

    1999   *Testing Women, Testing the Fetus: The Social Impact of Amniocentesis in America.* New York: Routledge.

Ravussin, Eric, Mauro E. Valencia, Julian Esparza, Peter H. Bennett, and Leslie O. Schulz

    1994   Effects of a traditional lifestyle on obesity in Pima Indians. *Diabetes Care* 17:1067–1074.

Reece, E. Albert, and John C. Hobbins

    1986   Diabetic embryopathy: Pathogenesis, prenatal diagnosis and prevention. *Obstetrics and Gynecological Survey* 41:325–335.

Reid, Barbara V.
  1992   "It's like you're down on a bed of affliction": Aging and diabetes
         among black Americans. *Social Science & Medicine* 34:1317–1323.
Reid, Raymond, and Everett R. Rhoades
  2000   Cultural considerations in providing care to American Indians. In
         *American Indian Health: Innovations in Health Care, Promotion, and
         Policy,* edited by Everett R. Rhoades, 418–425. Baltimore: Johns
         Hopkins University Press.
Ritenbaugh, Cheryl Kay
  1974   The Pattern of Diabetes in a Pima Community. Unpublished Ph.D.
         dissertation, Department of Anthropology, University of Califor-
         nia, Los Angeles.
Rock, Melanie
  2003   Sweet blood and social suffering: Rethinking cause-effect relation-
         ships in diabetes, distress, and duress. *Medical Anthropology*
         22(2):131–174.
Roseman, J. M.
  1985   Diabetes in Black Americans. In *Diabetes in America* (National In-
         stitutes of Health Publication no. 85-1468), edited by the N.D.D.
         Group, VIII, 1–24. Washington, DC: U.S. Government Printing
         Office.
Rust, Orion A., James A. Bofill, Michael E. Andrew, Tessa A. Kincaid, Thomas
M. Stubbs, Edith H. Miller, and John C. Morrison
  1996   Lowering the threshold for the diagnosis of gestational diabetes.
         American Journal of Obstetrics & Gynecology 175:961–965.
Sallis, James F. Jr., Melbourne F. Hovell, C. Richard Hofstetter, J. P. Elder,
Mimi Hackley, Carl J. Caspersen, and Kenneth E. Powell
  1990   Distance between homes and exercise facilities related to fre-
         quency of exercise among San Diego residents. *Public Health Re-
         ports* 105:179–185.
Sargent, Carolyn, and Joan Rawlins
  1991   Factors influencing prenatal care among low-income Jamaican
         women. *Human Organization* 50(2):179–187.
Scheder, Jo C.
  1988   A sickly-sweet harvest: Farmworker diabetes and social equality.
         Medical Anthropology Quarterly 2(3, Health and Industry):251–
         277.
Scheper-Hughes, Nancy
  1989   The human strategy: Death without weeping. *Natural History,*
         October:8–16.
  1991   The subversive body: Illness and the micropolitics of resistance.
         Anthropology UCLA. Special issue:43–70.

Schmidt, Maria I., Bruce B. Duncan, Angela J. Reichelt, Leandro Branchtein, Maria C. Matos, Adriana Costa e Forti, Ethel R. Spichler, Judith M.D.C. Pousada, Margareth M. Teixeira, and Tsuyoshi Yamashita
    2001   Gestational diabetes mellitus diagnosed with a 2-h 75-g oral glucose tolerance test and adverse pregnancy outcomes. *Diabetes Care* 24:1151–1155.
Schoenberg, Nancy E.
    1997   A convergence of health beliefs: An "ethnography of adherence" of African American rural elders with hypertension. *Human Organization* 56(2):174–181.
Schoenberg, Nancy E., Cheryl H. Amey, and Raymond T. Coward
    1998   Stories of meaning: Lay perspectives on the origin and management of noninsulin dependent diabetes mellitus among older women in the United States. *Social Science & Medicine* 47:2113–2125.
Schraer, Cynthia D.
    1994   Diabetes among the Alaska Natives—The emergence of a chronic disease with changing life-styles. In *Diabetes as a Disease of Civilization: The Impact of Culture Change on Indigenous Peoples,* edited by Jennie R. Joe and Robert S. Young, 169–193. New York: Mouton de Gruyter.
Schwartz, Martin L., Wendy N. Ray, and Suzanne L. Lubarsky
    1999   The diagnosis and classification of gestational diabetes mellitus: Is it time to change our tune? *American Journal of Obstetrics & Gynecology* 180:1560–1571.
Shapiro, Jason S.
    1997   Non-insulin-dependent diabetes mellitus among American Indians: A problem in human ecology. *American Indian Culture and Research Journal* 21(2):197–227.
Shattuck, Petra, and Jill Norgren
    1991   *Partial Justice: Federal Indian Law in a Liberal Constitutional System.* New York: Berg.
Sievers, Maurice L., Robert G. Nelson, William C. Knowler, and Peter H. Bennett
    1992   Impact of NIDDM on mortality and causes of death in Pima Indians. *Diabetes Care* 15:1541–1549.
Simon Eisner and Associates
    1973   *Gila River Indian Community Capital Improvement Program 1973–1977.* Tucson, AZ: Simon Eisner and Associates.
Singer, Merrill
    1990   Reinventing medical anthropology: Toward a critical realignment. *Social Science & Medicine* 30:179–187.

Skelly, Anne H.

    2002   Elderly patients with diabetes: What you should ask your patient on the next visit. *American Journal of Nursing* 102(2):15–16.

Smith, Cynthia J., Elaine M. Manahan, and Sally G. Pablo

    1994   Food habit and cultural changes among the Pima Indians. In *Diabetes as a Disease of Civilization: The Impact of Culture Change on Indigenous Peoples,* edited by Jennie R. Joe and Robert S. Young, 407–433. New York: Mouton de Gruyter.

Smith-Morris, Carolyn

    2004   Reducing diabetes in Indian country: Lessons from the three domains influencing Pima diabetes. *Human Organization* 63(1):34–46.

    2006   Community Participation in Tribal Diabetes Programming. *American Indian Culture and Research Journal* 30(2).

Sobal, Jeffery, and Albert J. Stunkard

    1989   Socio-economic status and obesity: A review of the literature. *Psychological Bulletin* 105:260–275.

Sobngwi, E., P. Boudou, F. Mauvais-Jarvis, H. Leblanc, G. Velho, P. Vexiau, R. Porcher, S. Hadjadj, R. Pratley, P. A. Tataranni, F. Calvo, and J. F. Gautier

    2003   Effect of a diabetic environment in utero on predisposition to type 2 diabetes. *Lancet* 361(9372):1861–1865.

Spikmans, F.J.M., J. Brug, M.M.B. Doven, H. M. Kruizenga, G. H. Hofsteenge, and M.A.E. van Bokhorst-van der Schueren

    2003   Why do diabetic patients not attend appointments with their dietician? *Journal of Human Nutrition and Dietetics* 16:151–158.

Stepan, Nancy Leys

    1993   Race and gender: The role of analogy in science. In *History of Women in the Sciences. Selections from Isis,* edited by Sally Gregory Kohlstedt, 269–285. Chicago: University of Chicago Press, 1999.

Stock, Robert

    1986   "Disease and development" or "the underdevelopment of health": A critical review of geographical perspectives on African health problems. *Social Science & Medicine* 23(7):689–700.

Szathmary, Emoke J. E.

    1993   Application of our understanding of genetic variation in Native North America. In *Genetics of Cellular, Individual, Family, and Population Variability,* edited by Charles F. Sing and Craig L. Hanis, 213–238. New York: Oxford University Press.

Szreter, Simon

    1997   Economic growth, disruption, deprivation, disease, and death: On the importance of the politics of public health for development. *Population and Development Review* 23(4):693–728.

Szurek, Jane

    1997   Resistance to technology-enhanced childbirth in Tuscany: The political economy of Italian birth. In *Childbirth and Authoritative Knowledge: Cross-Cultural Perspectives,* edited by Robbie Davis-Floyd and Carolyn F. Sargent, 287–314. Berkeley: University of California Press.

Tannahill, Reay
    1988   *Food in History.* New York: Three Rivers Press.

Terry, Jennifer
    1989   The body invaded: Medical surveillance of women as reproducers. *Socialist Review* 19:13–43.

Testa, Marcia, Johanna Hayes, Ralph Turner, and Donald Simonson
    2003   Obesity in type 2 diabetes is associated with reduced quality of life. *Diabetes* 52:A39.

Thomas, Lewis
    1983   *The Youngest Science: Notes of a Medicine Watcher.* New York: Penguin.

Tripp-Reimer, Toni, Eunice Choi, Lisa Skemp Kelley, and Janet C. Enslein
    2001   Cultural barriers to care: Inverting the problem. *Diabetes Spectrum* 14(1):13–22.

Townsend, Peter, and Nick Davidson
    1988   *Inequalities in Health: The Black Report.* London: Penguin Books.

Underhill, Ruth
    1979   *Papago Woman.* Prospect Heights, IL: Waveland Press.

U.S. Bureau of the Census
    2000   Demographic data, 2000. Electronic document http://factfinder.census.gov, accessed December 15, 2005.

U.S. Department of Health and Human Services
    1991   *Healthy People 2000: National Health Promotion and Disease Prevention Objectives.* Washington, D.C.: U.S. Government Printing Office.
    2000   *Healthy People 2010,* 2nd ed. 2 vols. Washington, D.C.: U.S. Government Printing Office.

U.S. Preventive Services Task Force
    2003   Screening for gestational diabetes mellitus: Recommendations and rationale. *American Family Physician* 68:331.

Valdmanis, Vivian, David W. Smith, and Myrna R. Page
    2001   Productivity and economic burden associated with diabetes. *American Journal of Public Health* 91:129–130.

van der Pligt, Joop
    1998   Perceived risk and vulnerability as predictors of precautionary behaviour. *British Journal of Health Psychology* 3:1–14.

VanItallie, Theodore B., and Albert J. Stunkard
    1990   Using nature to understand nurture. *American Journal of Public Health* 80:657–658.

Waitzkin, Howard B., and Barbara Waterman
  1974   *The Exploitation of Illness in Capitalist Society.* New York: Bobbs-Merrill.
Weaver, Thomas
  1973   Social and economic change in the context of Pima-Maricopa history. In *Atti del XL Congresso internazionale degli americanisti, Roma-Genova, 3–10 settembre 1972,* edited by T. Weaver. Genova: Tilgher.
Weidman, Dennis W.
  1987   Type II diabetes mellitus, technological development and the Oklahoma Cherokee. In *Encounters with Biomedicine: Case Studies in Medical Anthropology,* edited by Hans A. Baer, 43–71. New York: Gordon and Breach.
Weinberger, Morris, Stuart J. Cohen, and Steven A. Mazzuca
  1984   The role of physicians' knowledge and attitudes in effective diabetes management. *Social Science & Medicine* 19:965–969.
Weiss, Barry D., Janet H. Senf, and Wendy Udall
  1989   No relationship between pregnancy complications and variations in blood glucose levels among nondiabetic women. *Journal of Family Practice* 29:389–395.
Weiss, Kenneth M.
  1985   Diseases of environmental transition in Amerindians and related peoples. *Collegium Anthropologicum* 9(1):49–61.
Weiss, Kenneth M., Jan S. Ulbrecht, Peter R. Cavanagh, and Anne V. Buchanan
  1989   Diabetes mellitus in American Indians: Characteristics, origins and preventive health care implications. *Medical Anthropology* 11:283–304.
Weismantel, Mary J.
  1997   Time, work-discipline and beans: Indigenous self-determination in the Northern Andes. In *Women and Economic Change: Andean Perspectives,* edited by Ann Miles and Hans Buechler, ch. 3. Arlington, VA: American Anthropological Association.
Weiss, Peter A. M., Martin Haeusler, Franz Kainer, Peter Purstner, and Josef Haas
  1998   Toward universal criteria for gestational diabetes: Relationships between seventy-five and one hundred gram glucose loads and between capillary and venous glucose concentrations. *American Journal of Obstetrics & Gynecology* 178:830–835.
Wellbery, Caroline
  2003   Active role in diabetes care improves patient satisfaction. *American Family Physician* 67:877.

Wendorf, Michael
    1989   Diabetes, the Ice Free Corridor, and the Paleoindian settlement of North America. *American Journal of Physical Anthropology* 75:503–520.

Wendorf, Michael, and Ira D. Goldfine
    1991   Perspectives in diabetes: Archaeology of NIDDM, excavation of the "thrifty" genotype. *Diabetes* 40:161–165.

Western Management Consultants, Inc.
    1963   *The Industrial Development Potential of the Gila and Salt River Indian Reservation.*

Wiedman, Dennis William
    2001   Fat content of South Florida Indian frybread: Health implications for a pervasive Native-American food. *Journal of the American Dietetic Association* 101:582–585.

Williams, Clare
    2000   Doing health, doing gender: Teenagers, diabetes and asthma. *Social Science & Medicine* 50:387–396.

Williams, Desmond E., William C. Knowler, Cynthia J. Smith, Robert L. Hanson, Janine Roumain, Aramesh Saremi, Andrea M. Kriska, Peter H. Bennett, and Robert G. Nelson
    2001   The effect of Indian or Anglo dietary preference on the incidence of diabetes in Pima Indians. *Diabetes Care* 24:811–816.

Williams, Gareth
    2001   Diabetes black spots and death by postcode: The incidence, and inequity, of diabetes are likely to be worsened. *British Medical Journal* 322:1375.

Willoughby, Deborah F., Carolyn C. Kee, Alice Demi, and Veronica Parker
    2000   Coping and psychosocial adjustment of women with diabetes. *Diabetes Educator* 26(1):105–112.

Wilson, Robert, Carol Graham, Karmen G. Booth, and Dorothy Gohdes
    1994   Community approaches to diabetes prevention. In *Diabetes as a Disease of Civilization: The Impact of Culture Change on Indigenous Peoples,* edited by Jennie R. Joe and Robert S. Young, 495–503. New York: Mouton de Gruyter.

Wolf, Eric R.
    1982   *Europe and the People Without History.* Los Angeles: University of California Press.

Wolpert, Howard A., and Barbara J. Anderson
    2001   Management of diabetes: Are doctors framing the benefits from the wrong perspective? *British Medical Journal* 323:994(3).

Womack, Ranae Bohan
    1995   Beliefs of Native American patients about diabetes. *IHS Provider* 20(6):80–82.

Yawn, Barbara, Stephen J. Zyzanski, Meredith A. Goodwin, Robin S. Gotler, and Kurt C. Stange
    2001   Is diabetes treated as an acute or chronic illness in community family practice? *Diabetes Care* 24:1390.

Young, T. Kue
    1996   Obesity, central fat patterning and their metabolic correlates among the Inuit of the central Canadian Artic. *Human Biology* 68:245–263.

Zimmet, Paul Z., K.G.M.M. Alberti, and Jonathan Shaw
    2001   Global and societal implications of the diabetes epidemic. *Nature* 414:782–787.

Zimmet, Paul Z., R. L. Kirt, and Susan W. Serjeantson
    1995   Genetic and environmental interactions for non-insulin-dependant diabetes in high prevalence Pacific populations. In *The Genetics of Diabetes Mellitus* (Serono Symposium no. 47), edited by J. Köbberling and R. Tattersall. New York: Alan R. Liss.

Index

About the Author

Carolyn Smith-Morris has her B.A. in anthropology from Emory University, an M.S. in rehabilitation services from Florida State University, and her M.A. and Ph.D. in anthropology from the University of Arizona. She is now an assistant professor of anthropology at Southern Methodist University. Her ethnographic work addresses chronic disease and the health impacts of culture change on native and developing communities. Most of her research in the last nine years has been among the Pima (Akimel O'odham) Indians of southern Arizona. She has published education modules on diabetes for community health representatives and is at work on an ethnographic video for employees of the Gila River Health Care Corporation. She has also worked among the Wiradjuri Aborigines of New South Wales, in urban settings among Mexican immigrants, and among the elderly and dying on questions of end-of-life care and the Living Will. In 2004, she published an award-winning paper in *Human Organization* on the history, culture, and genetics behind Pima diabetes. Her 2005 article in *Medical Anthropology* addresses the complexity surrounding the diagnosis and treatment of diabetes and the implications of this evolving knowledge for patients. She has several other published articles and book chapters. This is her first monograph.